**ROCK
MUSIC**

ROCK MUSIC

BY BRIAN VAN DER HORST

FRANKLIN WATTS, INC., NEW YORK, 1973

◄—— A FIRST BOOK ——►

Cover by Jill Schwartz

Photographs courtesy of:
Atco Records – 41 (bottom); Atlantic Records – 42,
64, 84; Capitol Records – 58; Chess Records – 9, 23
(lower left); Columbia Records – 45; Decca Records –
6, 55; Farb, Nathan – 36, 63; *Hair* – 70; Levine, Anne
– Frontispiece, 69; Polydor Records – 41 (left); R.C.A.
Records – 14; United Press International – 23 (lower
right), 28, 35, 41 (right), 50, 79, 80, 86; Warner Bros.
Records – 23 (upper right).

Library of Congress Cataloging in Publication Data
Van der Horst, Brian.
    Rock music.
    (A First book)
    SUMMARY: A history of and guide to rock music,
from its origins in the blues to today's acid music.
    Bibliography: p.
    1. Rock music–Juvenile literature. [1. Rock mu-
sic] I. Title.
ML3930.A2V335   784   73-4959
ISBN 0-531-00789-8
ISBN 0-531-02419-9 (pbk)

TABLE OF CONTENTS

For all the
artists, friends, and
music people
who could not fit
into these few pages.

INTRODUCTION

This is not a book about today's music. It is written as a guide to the popular music of yesterday and tomorrow. There is no way that a book can accurately describe the rock music to which you are currently listening. It changes so quickly that not even the daily newspapers can keep up with the newest trends.

There is one thing, however, that all rock music has in common: its sources. Practically all the music we hear today has evolved from the blues and country music of the twentieth century. In fact, some of the oldest blues frequently reappear in new records that are hailed as the "latest" rock styles.

Rock music also revolves in distinct cycles. The music is alternately fast or slow tempoed. Various instruments pass in and out of favor, and the styles of performance alternate between big bands, small groups, and individuals.

This book is intended to serve as a handbook of rock music styles as they have entered and become part of the tradition of popular music. Hopefully, it will also serve as a manual for creative listening, as a field guide which will enable you to understand and appreciate the music you will be listening to when you read this book, whether it be in 1975 or 1995.

This is also a book about people. And what people! People who use music to reveal their deepest emotions. People who must live under incredible pressures, who must always be intensely present and creative. This is also a book to make you wonder and rejoice over the many people who can create an art form that is so clearly an expression of pure emotion and complete communication.

There is one undeniable reason for studying rock: it is the emotional record of our times, an indicator and signpost of past, present, and future directions of our spirit, humanity, and existence. It reflects the nature and concerns of the way we have lived. And as in any revolutionary and quickly changing form of art, it often provides new avenues for expressing human feelings.

But the main reason people listen to, buy, and play rock music is that it makes them feel good.

ROCK 'N' ROLL IS JUST A DIRTY WORD FOR BLUES

The term "rock 'n' roll" had been around for a long time before anybody really noticed it. The expression had been used in countless old blues songs since the turn of the century. Springing from the simple usage of "rocking in the cradle," the word rocking has always referred either to the motions ⸱ of dancing.

Early examples of the term in postblues songs were Roy Brown's 1947 hit of "Good Rockin' Tonight," "Rock All Night Long" in 1948, and "We're Gonna Rock" in 1951. By 1952 radio disc jockeys were announcing rhythm and blues (R & B) music as "that rocking and rolling sound." The same year, Allen Freed, a Cleveland disc jockey, started to add rhythm and blues records to his pop music radio show. The response from the kids was so overwhelming that he changed the name of his show to "Moondog's Rock and Roll Party." When he moved his show to New York City in 1954 and also started to promote concerts by R & B artists, the phrase was here to stay. Since no one had thought to apply the term "rock 'n' roll" to radio programs, newspaper advertisements, or theater marquees before, Freed is generally credited with coining the term.

But it was only a term. Much of the music of the late 1940's was identical with the rock 'n' roll hits of a decade later. While the music was steadily gaining one of the largest audiences in the world, no one in the business paid much attention. From the beginning, rock was a common pleasure and a cultural orphan.

But by the summer of 1954 — the boom year of rock 'n' roll — people began to take notice. This was the year that pop singers like Frank Sinatra, Perry Como, and Bing Crosby really began to wonder what was happening.

This was the year the Crows warbled "Gee," and the Chords sang "Sh-Boom" — two songs that are usually thought of as the first major examples of rock 'n' roll. Again, they were familiar music to rhythm and blues audiences. They contained much of the same mixture of blues and big beat, loud bass and drums, and strong rhythms attached to jazz riffs that had characterized R & B for over a decade.

What makes "Gee" and "Sh-Boom" conspicuous is that they sold records. They were the first examples of R & B music to be played on national popular radio stations. Before then, R & B could only be heard on small, independently-owned stations and could only be purchased on records in the black sections of major cities.

Starting with these two songs, young Americans could buy and hear the music they wanted throughout the country.

Other rock 'n' roll classics offered in 1954 included "Earth Angel," by the Penguins; "Work With Me Annie," recorded by Hank Ballard and the Midnighters; the immortal "Rock Around the Clock," initially released by Bill Haley and the Comets; and "Shake, Rattle and Roll," originally sung by Joe Turner.

But of course nobody in the pop music business was worried about this weird, novelty music. After all, Eddie Fisher, Rosemary Clooney, and Perry Como were still selling more records than anybody else. Then.

If we are to have any understanding of the nature of rock, we should first learn a little about the blues. The very music, drive, and spirit of rock is so much the musical child of the blues that from time to time, old blues become "new" rock hits.

The blues is the musical marriage between African and American folk song traditions. It is the rhythms, sounds, and scales of the African people — who first came to America as slaves in the seventeenth century — wed to the words and melodies of white folks — who brought their traditions to the United States and the Western Hemisphere from the British Isles and Europe.

Originally the blues were a form of communication in the fields. Before the Civil War, black slaves were not allowed to speak to each other while working on the plantations of the South. But their overseers allowed singing. The blues, therefore, started as work songs, accompanying the rhythm of a hoe digging a furrow in the field, a man bending and lifting to harvest a crop, or the blow of a hammer driving railroad spikes.

Black people, however, also used these songs to speak to each other. One would call out a question, and receive a response from a friend. This call and response style is the structure of the blues even today.

After the Civil War, these songs became more of a party and entertainment music in the South, and instead of just accompanying work rhythms, told stories and became a music of personal expression.

At the turn of the century the word "blues" appeared in many song titles, but the first published blues was not printed until 1912, with Hart Wand's "Dallas Blues." W. C. Handy usually gets the

In 1954 Bill Haley became the first rock 'n' roll star
after recording "Rock Around the Clock" with his group, the Comets.

credit for his "Memphis Blues," which was not exactly what we musically call a blues — it was more of a pop song. But as we'll see time and again in the history of music, it was remembered because it sold better than any of the competition.

The scale of blues includes "blue notes," which tend to give the music a ghostly or mournful quality. The chord structure of the blues is standard for much of rock 'n' roll even today — and was the rule for the first decade of rock.

Just before World War I, there were two mainstreams of blues: country and city blues. The country blues usually were autobiographical guitar songs sung by individual singers rather than groups. Many were men from the Mississippi River delta in Louisiana, like Robert Johnson, Bukka White, and Son House, who sang wailing, heavily chorded music. Others, like Blind Lemon Jefferson and Lightnin' Hopkins, who sang single-note-style melodic blues, were from the Southwest. And the men from the eastern seaboard sang a combination of black and white folk music — people like Blind Boy Fuller, Brownie McGhee, and Sonny Terry.

The country blues were also played by small string bands, who derived their style from the British folk music tradition and by jug bands, like the Memphis jug bands of Gus Cannon and Will Shade. There were also larger, traveling bands like the Rabbit Foot Minstrels and other variety shows that gave ensemble performances of the blues.

Then there were the blues that were sung in the cities. Most of the urban styles derived from the country blues, and are most often explained in terms of changing to hard, electric styles as they moved northward along the Mississippi River.

When the blues hit St. Louis, W. C. Handy and female singers like Bessie Smith and Ma Rainey, along with male singers like Lonnie Johnson, Tampa Red, and Leroy Carr, started adding jazz and horn arrangements that the blues had picked up from New Orleans.

By the time the blues reached Chicago, drums, saxophones, and bass were added, and most important of all the guitar was electrified, primarily so that it could be heard amidst the sheer volume of the other instruments.

By this time the music of black people was no longer merely called the blues. The heavy beats and large sounds, the deep bass rhythms of the urban bands were now something special. The music was recorded and generally referred to as "race" or "sepia" records. In the late 1940's, the music industry publication *Billboard* decided that the term was distasteful. They polled record manufacturers for an appropriate substitute. Around 1947, they came up with the name "rhythm and blues."

Some of the first rhythm and blues singers were basically country blues singers with electrified instruments; they might be using new arrangements, but they were singing the same old country way. These were people like Muddy Waters, whose R & B hit, "Rollin' Stone," inspired the name of the rock group led by Mick Jagger. Others, like Jimmy Reed ("Goin' to Kansas City"), John Lee Hooker, and Howlin' Wolf also wrote songs that later became hits as "rock 'n' roll."

When R & B went on to the big time in the 1940's it also meant big groups of musicians, and some of the earliest musicians started with several kinds of bands. Many bands, like those of Cootie Williams, Joe Turner, Lionel Hampton, and Billy Eckstine, were playing a mixture of jazz, pop, and R & B. Some of the earliest R & B revue shows of the '40's, such as the Johnny Otis Show, featured vocalists like Willie Mae "Big Mama" Thornton, who remained active into the '70's. In the '50's big band people went on to record songs like Turner's '54 version of "Shake, Rattle and Roll" — later to be recorded as a "cover" record (frequently, a note for note copy of someone else's composition) by Bill Haley and the Comets. For Haley, it was rock 'n' roll, but for Turner, it was the R & B he had been playing for years.

Most of the big band blues were the kind performed in dance halls, and were usually shouted, screamed, or wailed above the music. Performers like singer-guitarist B. B. King, Howlin' Wolf, and singer-harmonica player Sonny Boy Williamson played a more intimate style of the kind you would expect to hear in nightclubs and bars. They would whisper and growl and scream the blues in a wide range of feeling and dynamics — both a soft and a loud sound depending on the emotion of the song. Others, such as Chuck Berry and Muddy Waters, laid down the lyrical format of R & B. Many of these club singers were left behind by the rock 'n' roll explosion of the '50's only to be rediscovered a decade later.

The rhythm and blues style that was closest to the brink of rock 'n' roll, however, was the jump, or boogie, band style. Walking with a boogie rhythm — or moving with the beat — from the Memphis

Muddy Waters. His music provided one of the foundations on which modern rock 'n' roll has been built.

jug bands, the jump combos included piano, guitar, bass, and drums to play the shuffling beat, with a horn or a soloist up front. Louis Jordan's Tympany Five was the chief innovator of this style, with "Choo Choo C'Boogie," released in 1942. T-Bone Walker, Roy Milton, Amos Milburn, and piano players like Fats Waller (who went on to straight rock 'n' roll) were the professors of this school of music.

As the jump bands laid down the rhythmic foundations for rock 'n' roll, and the club bands did the lyrical approaches, it was the time-honored segment of black music called gospel that most heavily influenced the style for singing and harmonizing rock 'n' roll. Gospel derives from the spirituals, the religious songs of the blacks, which are as old as the blues themselves. In rural areas, especially, most black people considered the blues a disreputable kind of music to sing. So it was that many black singers either got their start singing religious music, or else remained singers of the church to maintain an "honorable" profession.

Mahalia Jackson, though she occasionally tried some pop recording, truly defined the spiritual style of singing, which emphasized a lyrical solo voice above background music. Gospel, which stressed the harmony and intertwining of many separate voices, was popularized through the singing of "Sister" Rosetta Tharpe. A third form of black religious music was the "signifyin'" style of music, which originated with the style of many black preachers in the pulpit, as they would question and talk with their congregations during the service.

Many rock 'n' roll performers have sprung from and wisely used each of these singing techniques. James Brown began his singing in the gospel style, and quickly developed the intense emotional tone of gospel as the hallmark of his act. Little Richard (Penniman) and Wilson Pickett also began as gospel-blues singers, and both retained many of the preacher qualities in their singing.

The gospel styles were soon embraced by popular music. Pop singers like the Mills Brothers and the Ink Spots used many of the same harmonies that appear in gospel in a slick, studied style. But young groups like the Ravens, the Larks, and the Orioles (it was very popular to be a bird then) began to appear. The new style was basically patterned after the religious tradition, culminating, perhaps, with the Orioles' "Crying in the Chapel" in 1953, which fully interposed the gospel style with a steady, if slow, rock 'n' roll beat.

The stage was set, and all that had to happen was for a young group of black singers called the Chords to write a song in 1954 that combined the vocalizing of gospel with the instrumental and lyrical concerns of blues and the striding, shuffling rhythm of the jump bands. The song the Chords wrote was "Sh-Boom," which, though covered in a national hit version by the Crew Cuts, is generally accepted as the first true example of rock 'n' roll.

"Sh-Boom," in the version the Chords recorded, had it all. It contained a clear use of the voice as an instrument. It used bebop phrases like "ya-da-da-da-da" and set the pattern of styles to come. It had gospel harmony, and the piano-guitar-drums-sax rhythm and blues use of instruments that was to become standard in rock, and the drums and bass rhythm section of the jump bands.

With "Sh-Boom," people had finally noticed the new music, albeit with some alarm. Beginning in 1954, they began to see that rock 'n' roll was more than just another musical fad.

**ROCK STARTS
ROLLING:
1954 TO 1956**

Rock 'n' roll, the earliest form of rock as we now know it, doesn't really exist anymore. It has become a part of the folk tradition, as have much of the rural and early urban blues. The folk tradition absorbs various forms of popular music. Songs usually stay alive by the oral tradition — being handed down from generation to generation by word of mouth. Rock 'n' roll is part of the folk tradition despite its printed sheet music and phonograph records. Whereas fathers used to teach their sons old songs, musicians and rock bands now teach each other old material. They play and rework old records, in a changing, folklike process.

Much of what happened between 1954 and 1956 exemplifies the folk process of rock 'n' roll. In those two years rock 'n' roll was formed from rhythm and blues, quickly changed from a folk expression of urban peoples to a folk music style, and then became a popular music phenomenon.

One of the most influential changes in the recognition of this new form of music was in its stars; in the personalities that became the means for youth to identify with the sounds of rebellion called rock.

Oddly enough, the first rock 'n' roll star was perhaps the least suitable figurehead for rebellion: Bill Haley. By the fall of 1954, Bill Haley had made it big. He had recorded a successful cover version of Joe Turner's "Shake, Rattle and Roll." However, it wasn't his first hit. In 1951 he had recorded "Rock the Joint." The following year, his "Crazy Man Crazy" was even closer to the rock tradition. It had all the earmarks of country music with its easy vocals and twangy guitar, and the beat of R & B. He also recorded a tune called "Rock Around the Clock." Although first released in 1954, and quickly dismissed as just a novelty, the song was used in a 1955 movie called "Blackboard Jungle." "Blackboard Jungle" was about the life and crimes of juvenile delinquents in a big-city high school. Along with the popularity of "The Wild One," a 1951 film starring Marlon Brando, which was about rough motorcycle gangs, and "Rebel Without a Cause," a 1955 film starring the late James Dean, which spoke of the rejection, loneliness, and violence of being a teen-ager, "Blackboard Jungle" became an enormous hit and so did "Rock Around the Clock." The song really wasn't very good because it had fairly boring lyrics and rhythm, but it had an hysterical, frantic, danceable beat. Bill Haley's shouted voice was white enough so that it was

13

played on all the radio stations that didn't play the black rhythm and blues — even though the song had a distinctly R & B beat.

Also, people made a great fuss about "Rock Around the Clock." They used it as a frequent example of how unmusical and degenerate the "young people's" music had become. With parents saying how bad it was, it wasn't very hard for their children to call it good. The youngsters of 1955 had recently found a place in the sun with the title of "teen-ager." Never before had adolescents had a name of their own. Now they had their own music, and started buying records like crazy. Unfortunately, their ears were not yet attuned to the roots and realities of rock 'n' roll.

Just as the Chords's "Sh-Boom" had been covered by the Crew Cuts, many white groups recorded their versions of black R & B hits and set the pace for the 1954–56 era. In many songs, a white singer made a version of a black singer's composition "acceptable" for white radio stations.

Although these records were selling and making a name for rock 'n' roll, it wasn't until a young white singer named Elvis Presley came along in the mid–'50's that the term became famous.

While Bill Haley brought out the sound of the new music, he was far from the image that youth was seeking. He was thirtyish, married with five children, and downright chubby. As far as a symbol of youthful rebellion, Haley was about as violent as a soggy marshmallow.

Strangely enough, the man who replaced Haley as the king of rock 'n' roll also grew up in the musical tradition of rockabilly — that spunky mixture of country, and rhythm and blues.

Elvis Presley lived in the blues-laden farmlands of the Mississippi delta until his family moved to Memphis where he first began to hear the country and western sounds of the East Coast. Presley idolized the life of the road, and while boning up on rural rhythm and bluesmen like Arthur "Big Boy" Crudup, T-Bone Walker, and Howlin' Wolf, he worked as a truck driver.

Presley wanted to be a singer, so like many of the young boys of Memphis, he would learn a song and go down to the Sun Records Recording Studio run by Sam Phillips and cut himself a few demos (demonstration records) to send around to recording companies. One day in 1954 Sam Phillips heard Presley in his studio, gave him

Elvis Aaron Presley was born on January 8, 1935, in Tupelo, Mississippi.

some material to work on, and quickly signed him to a management contract.

His first record for Sun, "That's All Right" (a Crudup song), broke big on the Memphis charts, and Colonel Tom Parker bought Presley's management rights while keeping him on the Sun label. Subsequent releases like "Mystery Train" and "You're Right, I'm Left, She's Gone," led Presley to be acclaimed the top country and western newcomer of the year and gave him his own traveling revue.

By this time, Presley was already creating a storm in the South. He had been an ardent student of the R & B stars like Bo Diddley and Chuck Berry, and had noted their acrobatic styles of performing with deep attention. While he performed in the South, he started swaying and rocking his body in time to the music just as he had seen the rhythm and blues singers do it in the national tradition of southern gospel singers. Only this was the first time white audiences had ever witnessed the style. The crowds went wild.

Presley's recording contract was put up for auction in 1955. Every major record company was interested, and in December RCA Victor came in with the highest bid, paid the highest amount for a single singer in those days, and bought out his Sun contract and unreleased master discs for $40,000. In February of 1956, "Heartbreak Hotel" was released and went on to sell enough records for two Gold Records — representing sales of over two million records. In two years, Presley's records had sold over 28 million single copies. But what flabbergasted the entire industry was that they sold so fast. Number one records used to remain at the top for months, but new Presley records were charging up the sales charts to the number one spot every week.

Newspapers called Presley shameful, churches dubbed him "morally insane," and quite a few cities banned him as obscene. His dark, sideburned, good looks and lanky poise made Presley the sex symbol for which the record market had been waiting. And his air of tough sensuality made him the symbol of rebellion for which youth had been clamoring.

Strangely enough, those who knew him reported he was a shy, courteous gentleman, always addressing his elders as "sir" and being the model son to his family. But in his songs "I Want You, I Need You, I Love You," "Hound Dog," and "Don't Be Cruel" he put down women, snarled sex, and created a beat that was the most danceable thing around.

Practically by himself, Presley had kicked off 1956 as the year of recognition for rock 'n' roll. Despite his horrified detractors, Presley also made rock respectable. Rock made Presley rich. And if singing and prancing like a black rhythm and blues artist could make fortunes, then it was respected. Respected by businessmen; respected by kids who wanted to grow up to be rock stars; respected by mothers who loved Presley when they were young — and who would later buy guitars and spangled shirts for their sons.

Ultimately, Presley made it possible for white kids to move and dance on stage as black men had been doing for years. The difference was in how much money whites could make at it — because they were selling tickets to white audiences, who were taking decades to get interested in black performers and the roots of rock 'n' roll.

STYLES OF
ROCK 'N' ROLL

The year of 1956 has been called the vintage year of rock 'n' roll. It was not that this was the year in which the best, or the most important songs of rock 'n' roll were written, but it was the year in which the music solidified into separate and distinct styles. This was quite an unusual phenomenon for any kind of popular music.

From 1900 until the 1930's, popular music was the kind of "Peg O' My Heart," swoon-moon-in-June type of sentimentality characterized by the ballads and musical show tunes coming from an area of New York around Twenty-seventh Street that was later dubbed "Tin Pan Alley." The Tin Pan Alley sound started with '20's music by singers and small bands, but by the '30's developed into a more instrumental approach called "swing."

Then the big bands swept the country in the '40's, developing the formula of even the pop sensations of today: the lead vocalists who frequently became more popular than the bands with which they sang. Frank Sinatra, Bing Crosby, Perry Como, and many others all started in this fashion. This phenomenon led to the next obvious step: vocalists as solo stars. The singers who became famous during this period were many of the same stars who were still around to witness the birth of rock: Eddie Fisher, Dean Martin, Vic Damone, Frankie Laine, and Tony Bennett. Some, like Johnny Ray and Sinatra, inspired hysteria on stage and in their audiences that was to create a standard by which the whole country would be appalled. By 1956 the country was protesting rock 'n' roll as the worst thing since death and taxes.

In April, 1956, *The New York Times* reported several attempts by white southern church groups to have rock 'n' roll denounced as part of a plot by the National Association for the Advancement of Colored People to corrupt white southern youth.

Besides the frequent bans on performers like Elvis Presley, most national radio stations usually banned more of the sexy rock and R & B as obscene or downright smut. Censorship ran rampant over most classical rhythm and blues lyrics; and, in several midwestern cities, public record burnings took place.

But rock 'n' roll was the music the young people wanted. When major labels did not release this new style, the public bought it in millions from independent record companies. Parents hated the new music for its danceable beat, its frank lyrics, and its unconventional approach to emotions. For the very same reasons, their children bought it — and made it their own.

It is the very nature of rock to mix and borrow from all varieties of music, but by 1956, the music we came to know as rock 'n' roll derived from five distinct genres of blues and black dance music. For this discussion, we are indebted to Charlie Gillett, who in his definitive work on the development of rock 'n' roll, *The Sound of the City: The Rise of Rock and Roll* (New York, Outerbridge & Dienstfrey, 1970), gave us the first clear delineation of these styles.

A. Northern Band Rock 'n' Roll. This was the urban, frequently white music most conspicuously identified with Bill Haley, who actually set out to make a new kind of music rather than develop a specific folk style. An issue of the *New Musical Express* in 1956 quotes Haley as saying, "We decided to try for a new style, mostly using stringed instruments, but somehow managing to get the same effect as brass and reeds." It was this intent, plus his fusion of country and western, rhythm and blues, and Dixieland that focused on "Rock Around the Clock," and established a form of music that is still evident today. Northern band rock also covers most of the fusion products that were to follow, and created a precedent for combining styles to create a new musical form — a technique to be brought to fulfillment by the Beatles a decade later.

B. New Orleans Dance Blues. The sloshing, often quick-tempoed rhythms of rock pianist-composer-singers like Fats Waller, Little Richard, and Larry Williams were modeled on combinations of the old-style New Orleans jazz played by Louis Armstrong, King Oliver, Professor Longhair; the famous Dixieland bands; and the Mississippi delta blues boogie styles.

When Fats Domino, a huge, wonderfully good-natured piano player from New Orleans played his hits like "Blue Monday," "I'm Walkin'," and "Blueberry Hill," you could hear all the late-night dances and the old strident boogie-woogie beat.

But when Little Richard stomped on the piano in a ferocious hurricane of notes and flashing rhythms, it was the voice of rock hysteria incarnate. You could also hear the roots of the preacher blues and shouting gospel songs that are his heritage. On songs like "Tutti Frutti," "Long Tall Sally," and "Good Golly Miss Molly," he was pure ecstasy. A slightly built man, he first appeared in long baggy pants, a flashy jacket, and a thunderhead shock of greasy hair that was perhaps the model for Presley's pompadour.

C. Country Rock or Rockabilly. Rockabilly was launched by virtually one man. Sam Phillips owned recording studios and a label, Sun Records, in Memphis. Phillips, originally a blues fan, was first to record such blues greats as B. B. King and Howlin' Wolf. In an interview in 1965, Phillips stated that he had first fused country and western styles with the blues in an attempt to popularize the traditional blues. He called the style "rockabilly," and one of the first singers he recorded in this style was Elvis Presley.

Another of Phillips' new rockabilly stars was Carl Perkins, who authored and recorded "Blue Suede Shoes" years before Presley's hit version. Another performer with more of a country than a blues background was the man who would come to be known as "Mr. Country," Johnny Cash, who had his first big hit with the 1956 Sun release of "I Walk the Line." Much later, in 1970, virtually everyone in pop music went through a rockabilly phase, from Bob Dylan to the Rolling Stones.

The best of the rockabilly artists to come to public attention in the '50's were the Everly Brothers and Buddy Holly and the Crickets. Both small groups, they extended the 'billy side of the tradition with their country lightness and harmonies.

The Everly Brothers, Phil and Don, were closest to bluegrass in their singing. Their high, reedy harmonies on records like "Bye-Bye Love," "Wake Up, Little Susie," "Bird Dog," and "Cathy's Clown" became the standard for group singing to be heard later in the styles of the Beatles, the Beach Boys, Crosby, Stills and Nash, and many others.

Buddy Holly, who died an untimely death in a 1959 airplane accident only two years after leaving his Texas home for his debut as a country and western singer, composed and recorded some of the truly classic songs of rock 'n' roll. His "Peggy Sue," "That'll Be the Day," "Maybe Baby," and others, developed new idioms of using lyrics as instrumental variations of emotion. In "Peggy Sue," for instance, he repeated the name dozens of times, but each time with a different, evocative enunciation and phrasing that opened techniques to describe emotions in song that have been textbook examples for the groups of the '60's.

D. Chicago Rhythm and Blues. When the blues traveled up the Mississippi River to Chicago, it reached an all-time high point of energy and drive. Of all the rock 'n' roll styles, it has been Chicago rhythm and blues that has held together the mainstream in rock throughout the last two decades.

Developed by many of the original delta bluesmen like Muddy Waters, Howlin' Wolf, Elmore James, J. B. Lenoir, and James Cotton — who were among the first to take up electrically amplified instruments — Chicago R & B was first simply rural blues with a beat; a large, urgent, sock-it-to-'em beat over which the blues were shouted in noisy club bars. But with the addition of songs written about life in the city, a new style was formed.

Chuck Berry and Bo Diddley were both revolutionary guitarists. They originated new styles to be played in the format of electric blues bands that are the rule even today: two guitars, drums, electric bass, and a harmonica or a saxophone. But Berry and Diddley also wrote songs — very good songs.

Chuck Berry has been relegated a particular place of honor in the memories of most people who play rock 'n' roll. His songs, such as "Maybellene" (coauthored by disc jockey Allen Freed), "School Days," "Sweet Little Sixteen," "Rock and Roll Music," "Roll over Beethoven," "Too Much Monkey Business," and "Johnny B. Goode" are in the repertoire of nearly every rock singer alive. His style has not changed since 1955 and has remained a definition of electric rock. For his consistency alone, many dubbed him one of the true folk artists of rock 'n' roll.

Bo Diddley was the keeper of the beat. Many of his songs were built around only one chord. But his music with its "shave and a haircut, two bits" sound was the essence of the early rock 'n' roll beat. His songs, autobiographies like "Bo Diddley," "Who Do You Love?," "Hey, Bo Diddley" were recited in a sinister tone bearing almost deadpan melodies. But he had the beat — and listening to the Stones and Beatles of today, you can hear who he gave it to.

E. The Vocal Group Styles. Public moralists of the 1950's would probably have been horrified to know that rock 'n' roll, that "obscene" sound they were hearing on their radios, was the direct descendent of religious music. Yet, the sound of the '50's was predominantly the highly harmonized vocal singing that was the result of a musical marriage of gospel vocal styles and rhythm and blues arrangements.

Top left: Little Richard was the first of the "big screamers," yelling at the top of his seemingly indestructible lungs. He was the first self-dubbed "King of Rock 'n' Roll," and one of the first performers of glitter rock. Top right: The Everly Brothers. Bottom right: born in California and first employed as a hairdresser in St. Louis, Missouri, Chuck Berry started a voluminous list of hit records in 1955. Bottom left: Bo Diddley's autobiographical songs pounded out the beat that characterized early rock 'n' roll.

The very first rock 'n' roll song to make national airplay, "Sh-Boom" was in this gospel tradition of close harmonies, fervent basses, and soaring falsettos. The new and obvious use of the nonsense syllables in rock 'n' roll had background precedents in most postwar vocal music — from the "ba-ba-boo's" of Bing Crosby to the "ah-ah-ah's" of pop choir versions of church tunes.

The forerunners of this style were the Orioles, whose 1953 version of "Crying in the Chapel" (which incidentally began on the country and western radio play lists), started the soaring expression of the '50's group style.

The subsequent 1954 hits of "Sh-Boom" by the Chords, "Earth Angel" by the Penguins, and the hits in following years of such great songs of teen-age life styles as the Coaster's "Yakety-Yak," "Searchin'," and "Charlie Brown," closed the case: rock 'n' roll was a vocal style as well as a blues progression and beat.

4

THE
ADOLESCENT
YEARS:
1957 TO 1964

The middle years of rock, 1957 to 1964, after the blazing growth period of 1953 to 1956, represent the formalization of rock. The music ceased to be a largely folk commentary on urban life styles, and instead became a highly specialized form of business.

These were the years of decline for some. Elvis Presley's change during these years predicted what was to happen to countless other rock stars of the period. His music and his many motion pictures earned Presley a multimillion-dollar fortune, but his art drifted away from his roots in rockabilly and the country blues. He began to sing "middle-of-the-road" (MOR), easy listening tunes and ballads just before he was drafted into the army in 1958. He left, still the symbol of earthy rebellion in rock, but came back as a most polite, decent, businesslike pop performer.

The music also changed. Rock 'n' roll, the age of innocence — and much of its initial passion — was thwarted until the middle '60's when the Beatles arrived. Still, there were many notable talents recording in these years. The Everly Brothers, Chuck Berry, Buddy Holly and the Cricketts, Fats Domino, the Coasters, Lloyd Price, and the Beach Boys had many of their first and foremost hits during this period, but largely, it was a period of "trends," or passing musical fads.

The first and most prevalent trend in 1956–57 was toward "teen-age rock." These were the styles that were the essence of teen-age life: dances, maltshops, drag races, and of course, falling tragically in or out of love. The teen-ager's life had been a primary concern of rock lyrics from the very beginning, of course. There were always the songs that rhymed moon and June, and talked about the "Teen Angel," "Teen Queen," "Earth Angel," "At the Hop," "A White Sport Coat and a Pink Carnation" — practically anything that could happen to the teen-ager was deathlessly exploited in song.

Pat Boone, who began by covering rhythm and blues hits, was the very figurehead of teen-age rock: he was clean, God-fearing, and a respectable big-brother image from his crew-cut head to his white buckskin shoes. By 1967, his style and cover songs, such as "Ain't That a Shame," and "Tutti Frutti" had earned him a network television show.

By then the teen-aged rock stars themselves began to crop up, beginning with Ricky Nelson, sixteen, who was a television teen-ager on his family's weekly show, and started with such songs as "Be Bop Baby" and "A Teenager's Romance." Next there was Paul Anka, a Canadian in his early teens, whose plaintive and rather well-written songs of teen despair like "Diana," "(I'm Just a) Lonely Boy," and "Put Your Head on My Shoulder" sold more than thirty million records in five years, and made him America's youngest self-made millionaire.

These were also the years of the invented or synthetic singers. It all started with a network television show called "American Bandstand," hosted by another star in the Pat Boone mold of big-brother to the teen-agers: Dick Clark. The show, broadcast from Philadelphia, was the formula for rock 'n' roll shows on television: invite many kids to a record dance, occasionally bring on stars to mouth words or sing along with their records (since they could not duplicate the studio sound of their records in live performance), and fill in with panel discussions of new records and trendy patter. Television became a way to sell the records of these new performers.

Two performers, Frankie Avalon and Fabian, were manufactured into singing stars via "American Bandstand" even though they lacked the volume to be heard on recordings without a lot of help from studio equipment.

But not all of teen-age rock was this grim. The trend also brought forth the respected talents of Buddy Holly. "Party Doll" — his initial release — was as teeny as they come. So were the first 1957 hit releases of the Everly Brothers, "Bye-Bye Love" and "Wake Up, Little Susie." The Coasters released their hits during this period, and "The Great Pretender" was recorded by the Platters. Among the best teen-age music of all were the songs released during the late '50's by Chuck Berry — "Sweet Little Sixteen," "School Days (Ring! Ring! Goes the Bell)," and "Memphis."

Dances

Rock 'n' roll has always been essentially dance music. During the 1940's the jitterbug, the Lindy, and other popular dances of the time were generally considered to be both scandalous and black. The dances were part of the same jazz, swing, and bebop tradition in which the music had started.

During the '50's, the rhythm and blues musicians began creating a dazzling variety of dances. By the time the music was known as rock 'n' roll in the middle '50's, there were dozens. Some had the names of animals, like the Duck, the Pony, the Fish, the Monkey. Others took their names from song titles, such as the Watusi, the Hully Gully, the Funky Broadway, and the Boogaloo; or from ways to move, such as the Walk, the Jerk, the Stomp, and the Dip.

27

The jitterbug and the Lindy were contact dances. At some time during the dance, the two partners embraced. With the dances of the '50's, people seldom touched. Improvisation was the rule, and people just moved as their imaginations permitted.

But it was a song called "The Twist" that was to have the most profound effect on rock music. In 1960, when "The Twist" became a big hit, Chubby Checker began to do a number of national television shows, and high society had taken to doing the dance in the Peppermint Lounge in New York City. It was an explosion. The Twist had become fashionable. Joey Dee, the bandleader at the nightclub, had an extraordinary hit with "The Peppermint Twist," and in an ironic fashion, insured his own eventual failure in music. For when people began dancing and improvising dances in the fashion of The Twist, they wanted a wider variety of music to dance to — consequently a club like the Peppermint Lounge, which only had one or two live bands, was limited in its styles of music. The answer to the crowd's demands was to fire the band and play records instead — and the discotheque was born.

The Twist and discotheques remained fashionable for a decade, growing in every major city in the world. Toward the middle of 1970, however, another phase was entered — people began to return to the rule of the late 1940's — just listening.

People no longer went to ballrooms to dance but went instead to concert halls to listen. Discotheques closed down, and despite great numbers of people dancing in their seats in concerts, nightclubs became popular once more. Most likely, the next stage will be going back to contact dances — and then perhaps the cycle of popular dance styles will begin anew.

Above: the Coasters.
Below: "The Twist" was
a hit for Chubby Checker
during the summer of 1960,
although it was
originally released by
Hank Ballard and the
Midnighters in 1959.

FROM
FOLK MUSIC
TO
FOLK ROCK

Another trend was launched in 1957 — one that perhaps forever altered the course of rock. In 1958 the Kingston Trio sang their version of a Blue Ridge Mountain folk song about a man hanged for killing his girl friend. "Tom Dooley" went on to be a multimillion best-selling single record, and sparked a national audience for sophisticated, simple-harmonied folk songs.

Folk songs had been sung among café society people for many years, notably by such truly ethnic singers as Leadbelly, who sang the blues and breakdowns of the South; Woody Guthrie, who sang songs of social consciousness and ballads in the tradition of the West; and the Carter Family, who strummed string-band versions of Appalachian Mountain music. Popularizers such as Pete Seeger, the Almanac Singers, and Richard Dyer-Bennett brought the British ballad traditions to college campuses, where young men were trying to find "honest" and "pure" music for confusing and often hypocritical times.

Popular folk music filled that need, but changed as rapidly as did its audience. At first the folk movement had no effect on record sales, and certainly never contributed any hits to the 45 rpm singles market. Folk music seemed to be for adults. It was recorded on long-playing albums that were associated with the "good" classical, jazz, and pop music — rather than "that rock 'n' roll garbage the kids were buying."

Strangely enough, the folk movement was created by everything *but* actual folk music. The first folk music stars were the Kingston Trio, who played a very sophisticated, slick version of traditional music; Joan Baez, who despite her efforts toward an ethnic "purity" still sounded more like folk stylists such as Dyer-Bennett; and the infectious, well-harmonized and arranged Peter, Paul and Mary. But popular folk music was to have an invaluable effect on the course of rock. It gave us the lyric.

As you could "hear the words" in folk music (compared to the din of rock), you could soon hear them in the rock 'n' roll styles. When the Beatles began using folk forms and Bob Dylan began playing electric music, the most obvious difference effected by these and many other cross-over artists from folk to rock was in their respect for making the lyrics understandable.

An interesting offshoot of the folk music boom were the efforts of another small folk movement of this time — Calypso. The worksongs of the Caribbean became polished and popularized by artists like Harry Belafonte through songs like "Jamaica Farewell" and

"Day-O," and the Tarrier's version of "Banana Boat Song." Just like the truly ethnic American folk styles, the music of the West Indies was also given a high gloss of commercial arrangements before it was accepted by the buying public. Other West Indian musical forms such as the Ska and the Reggae were later to crop up in the early 1970's in songs by such diverse artists as Aretha Franklin ("Funky Nassau"), Paul McCartney, and Simon and Garfunkel.

Ironically, the "folk" music that sold the most during the folk boom of the early '60's was a depressingly slick version of ethnic recordings. And while the public was buying what was comparable to Pat Boone cover versions of Fats Domino tunes, the folk market kept crying for "authentic" music. The most authentic contemporary folk music at the time was being played on the R & B radio stations — such as the Chicago blues by Chuck Berry, B. B. King, and Howlin' Wolf — which most purists considered "too corrupt," because it was electric music.

Folk Rock and Onward
During the early 1960's, not much happened in the mainstream of rock until the arrival of the Beatles in 1964.

At the turn of the decade, rock 'n' roll was in a fairly low state. The payola hearings had just closed. The careers of many disc jockeys throughout the country ended because they accepted money to play certain records. The man who gave rock 'n' roll its very name — Allen Freed — was finished. The payola scandals have often been criticized for making an unfair attack on the most revolutionary music of the period — rock 'n' roll.

After all, bribes and kickbacks were time-honored American business practices — why were they so unacceptable in radio? Not that it was all that widespread, certainly no more than in the say, washer and bolt industry. But there was something else — rock 'n' roll was a force that threatened the balance of things.

So that was the beginning of the '60's: everyone was afraid of playing music that was too radical, and folk music was the thing of the moment.

Bob Dylan and Folk Rock
And then Bob Dylan came to town. It began as early as the fall of 1960, when Bob (né Zimmerman) Dylan trekked to New York to visit the ailing Woody Guthrie, his idol and one of America's most prolific folk poets and songwriters. Hanging around Greenwich

Village, he played in the folk coffee houses, and was signed to a recording contract.

When looking at the bulk of Bob Dylan's work, one can immediately see his profound affect on modern music; perhaps he is the most influential of any one singer-songwriter of our time. For that matter, listening to his albums is like hearing a catalog of popular music styles of the twentieth century. You can easily place his records in four separate piles, the songs of which will sound as though they were written by four different composers and performed by four individual vocalists.

In chronological order, the first pile would be that of a rural folk singer of the blues and mountain tradition. The second would represent the styles of urban rhythm and blues from Chicago blues bands to the many varieties of rock 'n' roll. In the third you would hear the crooning inflections and lyrical concerns of country and western music and the fourth would ring with a collection of pop sounds in the styles of contemporary balladeers — from jazz to piano bar music to soul.

For Dylan, despite his past links with protest, anarchic, and psychedelic movements is perhaps one of the most American contemporary composers — a one-man melting pot of styles, cycles, and influences. Dylan led and innovated many of the musical movements in which he was involved. But leader or follower, he truly reflected his times — as has always been the role of the folk singer.

With the debut of his fourth album, "Bringing It All Back Home," his fans were downright outraged. Dylan had begun to use electrical instruments, the bane of folk music, to accompany his songs. But electricity had come to Dylan's songs before this album. A West Coast group of rock 'n' roll musicians called the Byrds, formed in true California style with members from other parts of the country, had set Dylan's "Mr. Tambourine Man" to an electrical arrangement in 1965. They are thus credited with beginning the style now known as folk rock — a combining of folk tunes and lyrical concerns with the styles and instruments of rock 'n' roll. Their record of the Dylan song was a number one hit, but not for Bob Dylan.

When he sang "Blowin' in the Wind" at the 1963 Newport Folk Festival, he was the hit of the year, but when he tried to sing the songs from his new album on the same stage in 1965 with electrified rhythm and blues instrumentation, he was almost booed off the stage by his folk fans. They would only accept him with his harmonica on a mouth rack and playing acoustic guitar.

Folk rock was born, criticized, and accepted all in the same short year of 1965. What started in March with Dylan and the Byrds soon spread to groups like Sonny and Cher, the Turtles, and individuals like Barry McGuire ("The Eve of Destruction"), Donovan (at first a mimic of Dylan, but later a fine, original talent), and unique singer-songwriters like Richard and Mimi Farina, Tim Hardin, and Eric Andersen.

Had it not been for folk rock, Simon and Garfunkel might still be singing in "basket houses" — those clubs where artists are not paid salaries; the basket is passed among the audience for spare change after performing a set.

Instead, they became perhaps the most consistently successful of all the folk rock stars. In 1957, under the name of Tom & Jerry, Paul Simon and Art Garfunkel had a hit single — at the age of sixteen — with a record called "Hey Schoolgirl."

After that, nothing much happened for many years, until they recorded "The Sounds of Silence" on an album as part of the folk song boom of 1964. The song became a favorite of a New York disc jockey, who played it frequently on his radio show. Finally, a Columbia Records producer named Tom Wilson heard and liked the song enough to rerecord it with drums, bass, and electric guitar: rock 'n' roll accompaniment. The result was the number one smash hit released in January 1966.

The success of their following records provided them with more time to compose. Even though they did look a little like the cartoon characters of Tom and Jerry on stage, Simon the slight mouse, Garfunkel the long lithe cat, they were articulate, hip, and easily won the love of the college market.

Their songs were filled with the self-searching concerns of college and late adolescence, and coupled with truly inventive musical talents and the use of sentiment (versus sentimentality), they sold millions of records. Still, they did not become big-time artists until 1968, when they were asked to contribute music for the sound track of the Mike Nichols film, "The Graduate."

Above: Bob Dylan, a nineteen-year-old ex-rock 'n' roll singer from Minnesota, came to New York City and gave the contemporary folk ballad and blues tradition a new relevance and a new home — the city. Below: The artists who had perhaps the most influence in making folk rock recognized were two artists who had been dismissed as has-beens for nearly a decade: Simon and Garfunkel.

Folk rock was most important in the stage it set for 1966 — the dawn of electric art music. Many folk rock groups like the Buffalo Springfield, the Youngbloods, the Mamas and the Papas, and the Lovin' Spoonful; and many singers like Tim Buckley, Joni Mitchell, and John Prine created electric styles from acoustic "folk music." And although folk rock continued in the music of Crosby, Stills, Nash and Young; the Grateful Dead; and James Taylor; it was forgotten by 1967. Folk rock disappeared in the same pool of influences and styles that was to change rock 'n' roll from an ethnic music to an art form — as we will see in the next chapter.

James Taylor.
His songs truly illustrate
the lyricism of folk rock.

6

SOUL: FROM THE BEGINNING TO "BLUE-EYED"

The modern concept of soul actually started in 1954. It is blues fused to gospel, underpinned with the sensuous beat of rhythm and blues and illuminated with brass sounds reminiscent of the big bands. And the man who began it all was Ray Charles.

Charles first patterned his singing style after the smooth pop of Nat "King" Cole. He then began combining gospel approaches with R & B music. "I Got a Woman," one of his first big hits, resulted from that famed recording session of a blues based on the gospel tune, "My Jesus Is All the World to Me." Some old-time blues singers were appalled at how he joined a love song with sacred music.

But for Charles, it was the beginning of a long string of wildly successful records, including more than thirty best-selling albums. Among his most notable hits were "What'd I Say," "Hit the Road Jack," and "I Can't Stop Loving You."

Ray Charles' music is dominated by a piano and blues band sound. Many of his earlier recordings of the 1950's were pure rhythm and blues arrangements — but it was his gospel style and improvisations that created the soul genre of music, almost single-handedly.

Almost, for the man who was later to be known as "Soul Brother #1," James Brown, was also working as early as 1956, when his first big hit, "Please, Please, Please," broke the charts. If Charles developed the sound of soul, it was James Brown who keynoted its look. As Charles took the inflections and vocal styles of church singing, Brown took the signifying, hollering, ecstatic ways of tent-meeting southern religion and made it part of his act. A man of opulent wealth and style, Brown has never gone long without a hit record. Among his million-selling records are "Cold Sweat," "Prisoner of Love," "I Got You (I Feel Good)," "Papa's Got a Brand New Bag," and "Hot Pants."

Another black singer who grew up in the gospel tradition and began setting the pace for a more sophisticated soul that was to become popularized by such singers as the Supremes, Dionne Warwick, and Percy Sledge, was Sam Cooke. The son of a Baptist minister, his style of songs like his 1957 "You Send Me" and "Shake" were to influence soul greats like Otis Redding for years after Cooke's murder in 1964.

Ray Charles, James Brown, and Sam Cooke helped originate the soul styles of solo performers, but it was the Memphis Sound that set the pace for soul groups. The Memphis Sound were artists such as Booker T. and the MG's (Memphis Group), Carla Thomas, and eventually (perhaps the greatest soul performer of his day), Otis Redding.

When it came to the most sophisticated soul groups, it was an auto worker and songwriter from Detroit named Berry Gordy, Jr., who formed a music company that was to set the future pace. With $700 borrowed from his family's credit union, Gordy formed Motown Records (a contraction of Motor Town) and recorded his own song "Way over There" with Smokey Robinson and the Miracles, to a limited sales success. In 1961, however, with their first gold record, "Shop Around," Robinson became a triple treat songwriter, performer, and producer, and for Motown the "Detroit sound" was born.

In 1962 the Supremes, led by Diana Ross, released their first single on Motown, and set the pace for slick soul groups. The Supremes were phenomenally successful and sold over two million copies of "Where Did Our Love Go?" in 1964. They have sold a million copies of practically every record they have cut. Later in their career, they split into individual acts, but in the period of 1957 to 1964, they cut the original groove for sophisticated soul.

All that was left was for the world to recognize soul as a distinct art form. And 1964 to 1965, surveyed in the next chapter, provided the artists and the attention that were to create recognition of soul as *the* black blues form of the 1960's.

As history shows, most black music forms are traditionally ignored until they are suddenly discovered by white audiences — but only in acceptably watered-down, altered arrangements.

Soul reached its peak as a life force in music during the period of 1964 to 1966. During these four years, the people who had been working in rhythm and blues for decades became successful, well-known, and recognized for creating their unique brand of music — curiously at just the same time as white musicians were earning

Above right: blind from early childhood, Ray Charles learned music through braille and taught himself to play the piano, the trumpet, and the saxophone. He also taught himself to arrange and conduct music, even though hampered by a personal life full of struggle, poverty, and misfortune. Above left: James Brown built up each of his songs to a frenzy of emotions. Screaming, writhing, and shouting almost to the point of exhaustion, he established the spirit of the soul performer turning inside out for the audience. Below: Otis Redding was a proponent of the Memphis sound — the combination of repetitive rhythms from drums, bass, and guitar with melodies from brassy horns.

praise for music that they had borrowed from blacks. These were the years of Otis Redding, Aretha Franklin, the Motown complex, Wilson Pickett, Sly Stone, and finally — the phenomenon that was to wed soul and rock toward the end of the decade — blue-eyed soul.

It was the sound of Otis Redding and the Memphis Group back-up team that would be parodied in records later called soul rip-offs. But Redding and the label he worked on, Stax-Volt, was the largest body of soul-for-soul-sake, and included Sam and Dave, Carla Thomas, Arthur Conley, Joe Tex, and others. It was eventually the Stax label that brought the word "soul" to the top of the charts in the boom year of soul — 1967 — with tunes like "Soul Finger," "Soul Man," and "Sweet Soul Music." The Stax artists put the name soul where rhythm and blues formerly read as the label for professional black music.

The life of Otis Redding was typical of the music he sang. Born the son of a Baptist minister in Dawson, Georgia, he grew up in Macon — the same area as another gospel-oriented black singer, Little Richard. Indeed, much of Redding's performing style was reminiscent of Richard's "ecstasy" quality.

Redding would use all the hysteria-provoking crowd techniques of a gospel song leader to move his audiences. He would leap and shake around the stage as if possessed. He would shout phrases and commands over and over until the audience was chanting and moving along with him. As an entertainer, he was one of the most hypnotic.

On records, one of his first big hits was "Mr. Pitiful," as he was called for many years after. Then he began busting out with hits like "I've Been Loving You Too Long," and the Stones' "Satisfaction," and "Try a Little Tenderness." But one of his most effective hits was "Respect," which when sung by Aretha Franklin became the number one best-selling soul song of 1967. Just at his peak as an artist and a songwriter, Otis Redding had not yet become highly successful. At this time he recorded "Dock of the Bay," and then died in an airplane crash at the age of twenty-six before his next album was released. His song, and the succeeding album, "History

Aretha Franklin has been lauded and
placed in the same class as Bessie Smith,
Ma Rainey, and Mahaila Jackson — a singer's singer.

of Otis Redding," went to the very top of the music charts. But everyone sorrowed that the king of soul had left them before he had time to enjoy his crown.

These were also the years when Aretha Franklin exploded on the music scene. With the death of Otis Redding, she became the personification of soul. Another soul artist born to gospel, she sang in the choir of her father's New Bethel Baptist Church in Detroit. Born in Memphis, Tennessee, her mother left the family when Aretha was six and died four years later. This might account for Franklin's famed shyness. "I was afraid. I sang to the floor a lot," she would say about her early performing days.

Though first pushed in the direction of slick pop ballad singers, Franklin came to life with her very first single "I Never Loved a Man the Way I Love You." By going back to the black gospel roots, her singing took on that churchy funk and then enjoyed phenomenal success. Her next hits, "Baby I Love You" and "A Natural Woman," were instant classics. There was no other voice — male or female — that could compete with her soaring joy and dazzling improvisation. Everything that made the blues warm and exciting crept into Franklin's songs and were shot straight to the hearts of her audience fueled with gospel dynamite.

With her later records, Franklin has emerged as a talented songwriter; and her performing style has blossomed as well. Year after year, Franklin keeps getting better and better. Though still privately shy, her public performing style is now persuasive and wildly stimulating. Her stories and conversations with audiences leave crowds enthralled, in love with Lady Soul.

The East Coast has always been a seat of a unique selection of hard, bluesy, urban music. There has never been one coherent style arising from any of the eastern cities, but much of the music has been categorized as blue-eyed soul, or white musicians singing and playing black R & B music.

An outstanding talent to come from the soul movement in New York City was a solo female singer named Laura Nyro. She handles soul the way Dylan handles folk. She has taken the styles, vocal harmonies, and rhythms of soul music as a foundation on which to build her own style of poetic music. Though she uses the inflections

Laura Nyro.
A singer of blue-eyed soul.

and idioms of soul, she is a true original, having written such hits as "Stone Soul Picnic" and "Sweet Blindness" (ironically hits for a mostly black pop group, the Fifth Dimension).

For one of the finest, the Blues Project, much of this was true. They sang the rhythm and blues music of black America — but they sang it well. Consisting of Danny Kalb on vocals and lead guitar, Al Kooper on keyboards, Steve Katz on rhythm guitar, and others, it was one of those groups that seemed to have the best possible line-up and played the most sophisticated blues in years. Their few albums were critical successes.

The Lovin' Spoonful, led by John Sebastian, was another New York phenomenon who were proponents of the folk rock school. They were some of the best of the cheerful, elegantly funky rock with 1966 hits like "Do You Believe in Magic?" and "Daydream."

During this time, there were quite a few blues-oriented rock groups from the New York area like the Rascals, the Vanilla Fudge, and the Blues Magoos.

THE BRITISH

Had it not been for the Beatles, no one would have ever taken rock music seriously. While they were together, they gave rock standards of measurement and growth, and changed this dance music of the common city folk into a recognized form of art.

"I Want to Hold Your Hand" was released in America in January of 1964. Within ten days, there were orders for one million copies. By April, there were twelve Beatles singles among the top one hundred best-selling records in the country, and the top five were all Beatles.

Before the Beatles, rock 'n' roll had mostly wailed about the frustrations, pains, and obsessions of adolescent development. The song was in the first person ("I Couldn't Hide the Tears in My Eyes"), and the emotion was mournful. The Beatles brought an adult objectivity to the music along with a truly youthful point of view. They approached songwriting from the third person, telling stories in narrative form, and often in the second person — saying "she loves *you*" rather than "she loves *me*."

But two things were paramount in their importance and their success: primarily, they had fun. They sang happy songs in contrast to the sorrowful body of music around them. They had a ball and let everybody know it, every time they performed and in every song they wrote.

Secondly — and this was the gift by which they changed the course of popular music — they were skilled in a dazzling array of styles, and kept experimenting with new ones. For the large part of their career, they never repeated themselves. And whenever they did, they quickly lept forward in a new direction.

Paul McCartney was the sweet, superboyish one who not only appeared to be the group's spokesman, but being the one with the most universally regular features, also looked "the prettiest." John Lennon was the supersexy space cowboy: glasses, flip phrases, and a hip sense of comedy. He was the intellectual, the one who read the most and wrote the most (two books: *In His Own Write* and *A Spaniard in the Works*). On stage, John was the fire to Paul's sweet ice. While Paul would posture with exuberant dignity, John would swirl and charge, prance and leer, eyes rolling and hips shaking in the best of the rock traditions. Girls would sigh and ooh over Paul, but John would turn them inside out.

George Harrison was quiet on stage — not even given to the nods and little jumps of Paul. Sometimes he'd play off to the side —

as if he were playing to himself; always slow and deliberate, never seeming to have the bounce of the others. It was George who first united music from India with big-time rock 'n' roll. In the space between the first Beatles movie and their second, "Help!," he studied sitar in India with Ravi Shankar, composed a few songs implementing the droning lutelike instrument, and almost single-handedly fused a line of East-West musical interaction.

There was as much oriental influence in George's head as there was in his music. He became interested in the Eastern religions, in transcendental meditation — and after a while became the picture of a bearded, begowned mystic.

Ringo Starr had almost as many fans as Paul. While the rest of the group played up front, Ringo was locked to his set of drums upstage, and the best he could do was to throw the audience a goofy grin now and then. Born Richard Starkey, he had changed his name to Ringo Starr, and wore dozens of rings on his hands to reinforce the nickname. The last to join the band, he was always treated a bit like an outsider, but his sparkling dry wit and laconic humor quickly gave him his share of the Beatles' sunshine.

"A Hard Day's Night" was the capstone to the Beatles' commercial success (the sound track album of the film was released before the film: the sales of the album made back the cost of the film before it had ever been shown). Similarly, it was the album "Revolver" (released in August of 1966) that was the group's first triumph as artists.

What led up to this album? Early Beatles' albums were mainly collections of other composers' works with a few of their own original compositions. These albums established the objective style of their music — their songwriting genius did not gel until "A Hard Day's Night."

The "serious" Beatles, the Beatles as artists, began with the release of the single, "Ticket to Ride," in May of 1965. Equipped with one of the funkiest bass riffs in history, this song began perking up ears everywhere with the sheer musicianship of the Beatles. People started listening to the music instead of to the hysteria.

Up to this point, the musicianship of the four was standard — with one notable stylistic exception: their dynamics, how soft or loud they played. They constantly set the pace for future rock by always mixing their vocals and guitar above the rhythm section, giving a high, Everly Brothers-Buddy Holly clarity to their music. They also

began using their guitars — with Lennon on lead guitar, McCartney on bass, and Harrison on rhythm, as vocal instruments — in the best tradition of the country and Chicago bluesmen.

"Revolver" had everything that was later to distinguish the Beatles as artists both separately and independently. There was the cheerful nonsense of "Yellow Submarine"; the social comment of "Eleanor Rigby," with its baroque string quartet background; "Good Day Sunshine," with the classical influence of Bach; the exuberance of "Got to Get You into My Life"; and the psychedelia of "Tomorrow Never Knows."

The Beatles had made it. Everyone from Leonard Bernstein of the New York Philharmonic Orchestra to the *Paris Review* acclaimed them as having fused popular culture with classic art. As it turned out, it was only the beginning. But more about the Beatles when we get to their later works.

What had happened in the period we have just discussed, from 1964 to 1966, was that rock music made a name for itself. Not only could it be a commercially successful venture, but it was now also certified by both the media and intellectual establishment as a legitimate, if newly born, art form.

The British Invasion

With the success of the Beatles, many more English groups began to come to America. For a while, it seemed that every group from the Beatles' Liverpool birthplace that could lift a guitar would be imported to America. But most of them simply did not sell records.

The Dave Clarke Five was the first group to follow the Beatles to the United States — with their airplanes actually crossing in midair!

They were a cheerful, bouncy group — they even made a film in what was now another Beatles tradition. They had versatility instead of style, enthusiasm instead of composing energies, and were successful in lasting a few years without creating any major impact on contemporary music.

The Rolling Stones were the next significant band to cross the Atlantic. At the time, they lived in the shadow of the Beatles, but

When they arrived on their first whirlwind tour of America on February 7, 1964, the Beatles unleashed the happiest sound to hit rock in a decade.

as their musical identities crystalized, they were to walk on the waters of musical history as no group had ever done before.

But when Brian Jones, Mick Jagger, and Keith Richard started playing together (with Ian Stewart) in 1962, England had gone wild over the American rock 'n' roll greats of the '50's. By 1964, the rage in Britain was the Chicago bluesband styles of Chuck Berry, Muddy Waters, and Bo Diddley — who by this time had fallen on lean times in America.

It was in England that these same bluesmen became heroes and had the most successful tours and public appearances. So it was no wonder that the group who were to become the Rolling Stones would be playing the same music between 1962 and 1966 that had first given rise to rock 'n' roll itself: the electric urban blues.

By 1963, the band began an eight-month reign at the Crawdaddy Club in Liverpool. Mick Jagger, who sang lead vocals and played harmonica from the beginning, was the son of a physical education teacher, grew up in an average middle-class sort of way, and even attended the London School of Economics for a bit before dedicating himself to his stage career. His only previous working experience was as a physical education counsellor-instructor on a United Nations Service Base. Keith Richard was an art student, and first played with a country and western band before playing lead guitar and singing for the group. Brian Jones, who served on rhythm guitar, harmonica, and vocals worked in various odd jobs after a public school education. Charlie Watts, the drummer, had worked in an advertising agency and played in blues groups before joining the Stones. Bassman Bill Wyman was in the Air Force and then worked as an engineer. All five were fairly unremarkable chaps — until they began creating some very exciting rock 'n' roll.

The group as a whole looked like the meanest, filthiest, most sinister collection of street toughs you could ever meet in a nightmare. And their public behavior on and off stage fulfilled the promise of every scruffy thread they wore. The Stones were the last thing with which your parents wanted you to associate.

Jagger, as the lead singer and most frontally performing, conspicuous member of the group, did things on stage no audiences had ever seen a white man do before. He actually made Elvis Presley look tame. He pranced, minced, leered in a manic hysteria. He would   toss his tail in a bumpy grind to posterity — the posterity of the Rolling Stones.

Their first two albums were basically a salute to the blues and soul greats that they had revered most of their lives: including songs like Muddy Waters' "King Bee," Lieber and Stoller's "Under the Boardwalk," Chuck Berry's "Carol," and Willie Dixon's "I Just Want to Make Love to You." They wrote some fine songs in the blues tradition for these albums, but it was not until the release of "Out of Our Heads" that the songwriting team of Jagger and Richard became appreciated.

That incredible album contained what was surely one of the theme songs of the '60's — "Satisfaction," with the driving beat that was to be paramount in rock 'n' roll and a secret kept from all others who would try to make their kind of music. Also included was the magical "Play with Fire," setting up the prototype of the Stones' love song: the apposition of the society girl   with a London lower-class tough.

These were songs telling youth what was really happening. The honest and often raw sexuality of their songs made them a unique adventure in asexual popular music.

The musical identity of the Rolling Stones has always been untouchable by all their imitators, and has remained more constant in the changing world of rock than perhaps any other group: they had the beat. They made music with such a vamping, textural, sensual rhythm that it was and still is almost impossible to listen to their music without starting to move, beat time, dance. The incredible movement of their sound goes back to the beginning of music itself — to the time when music was an instinctual rhythm of life, sex, birth, and death.

Apart from the Beatles, the Dave Clarke Five, and the Rolling Stones, the British wave was populated by blues groups like the Animals, and cutesy groups like Chad and Jeremy and Herman's Hermits. Most of the first wave of English groups to America were to flash and then flow in varying degrees of decline. Two groups worth noting, however, were the Kinks and the Yardbirds — the Kinks were to make critically acclaimed but publicly tame recordings for the next eight years, and the Yardbirds were to be a nest for rock stars to come such as Jimmy Page, who was to form Led Zeppelin with most of the Yardbirds' personnel, and Eric Clapton, who was to create Cream. In retrospect, the Yardbirds were to become one of the most musically influential groups of the 1960's in England.

The British Are Coming . . . (Again)

The second wave in the English invasion of musical America, that is, the artists who arrived during the late 1960's after the first horde headed by the Beatles and the Stones, was probably initiated by the Bee Gees.

The Bee Gees arrived from England with their hit, "New York Mining Disaster — 1941," on which they sounded quite like early Beatles. The group, led by the Gibb Brothers — Barry, Robin, and Maurice — contributed a pop-opera "Odessa" to the scene.

Other second-wavers were the Hollies, whose lilting rock scored with "Carrie-Ann." Their leader, Graham Nash, went on to join Steve Stills and David Crosby in later years. Then there was the Incredible String Band, composed of Robin Williamson and Mike Heron. Between the two, they played an orchestra of instruments, and sang a sort of free-form music with strains and influences from everywhere — truly the most eclectic of the '60's groups. Procol Harum, whose classical sound was largely achieved by Matthew Fisher's organ work, created "Whiter Shade of Pale" and "Conquistador," two hit songs that were examples of baroque (piano-style) rock.

One of the longest-lived groups in rock also became prominent at this time, the Kinks. Peter Quaife, Mick Avory, Ray and Dave Davies, were in business since 1964, with "You Really Got Me." Characterized by an untogether stage presence they often gave disappointing tours.

The second British wave gave us three of the most important groups of all times: the Who, the Jimi Hendrix Experience, and Cream.

The Who — master guitarist-composer Peter Townsend, John Entwistle on bass, Keith Moon on drums, and Roger Daltry on lead vocals — were originally called the Highnumbers, and got together in 1963. In the mid-1960's in England a group had to be quite outstanding to get people to listen to its records. Peter Townsend attracted attention by wearing the first flag clothes. This was before anyone wore United States or English flags as clothing, so when he came out on stage with a Union Jack shirt he was an outrage.

Then at the Monterey Pop Festival in 1967 — where Janis Joplin was first acclaimed — they went into their act. At the end of their performance they smashed up everything on stage. Drums went flying, Townsend broke his guitar in great flailing circles of vengeance. Smoke bombs went off and total destruction reigned. After they had

The Who has done
many albums — all are
gems of rock 'n' roll.

made their expected hit, people began to notice that they were also very good singers and musicians.

They also wrote and performed the most successful concept album to date: *Tommy*, a rock opera about a deaf, dumb, and blind boy who seeks salvation playing pin ball. He finds it, and starts a new religion — but only after going through some of the catchiest narrative rock songs ever composed.

The late Jimi Hendrix was also discovered at the Monterey Pop Festival of 1967. Oddly enough, his act was also fraught with violence. He would leap and pump his guitar as he played his blues-oriented rock in the most suggestive of sexual manners. Then he would play his guitar on his back, stomp on it, finally play it with his teeth — but as the critics pointed out — tastefully. At the climax of his act he set his guitar on fire.

The Jimi Hendrix Experience consisted also of Mitch Mitchell on drums and Noel Redding on bass. Actually, Hendrix was born in Seattle, Washington, but only received recognition in this country after returning from England with his first album and the 1967 Monkees tour. Naturally, when mothers of Monkees fans saw his outrageous sexuality, he was thrown off the tour with much publicity.

Jimi Hendrix, one of the finest blues rock guitarists, was master of the feedback, wah-wah, and high volume school of rock. As happened to Jim Morrison of the Doors and Janis Joplin, the pressures of life as a superstar caught up with Jimi Hendrix, and in 1970 he died from an overdose of drugs, leaving behind work spread out through twenty-one albums — with unreleased posthumous works on the way.

Cream was also part of the late '60's blues explosion in rock. Eric Clapton, guitarist, Ginger Baker, drummer, and Jack Bruce, bass, were the three members — and each was considered a virtuoso on his instrument, hence their arrogant name. They played some of the best hard rock ever using electric amplification for heavy volume, and repetitive chords to create a powerful, textural sound.

Their rock was true improvisation. They would strive to rework a tune, stretch it, and draw new thought from it whenever they played. And they played anything. Basically a blues band, they experimented with Dylan tunes, delta blues, and jazz. They first got together in 1967, and were an inspiration to rock. After several years of delicate music and quasi-folk sounds, they brought the beat and the guts back to rock before they split up in 1968. And where did they get it? From the blues, of course.

CALIFORNIA:
THE SOUND
OF THE SURF

While the British were swarming over the eastern bulwarks of the American continent, another invasion was creeping across the country from the West. It originated in California, and you could hear it coming in the sound of the surf. Starting as a West Coast answer to East Coast teeny-rock — which centered on urban social pursuits of going steady, or to the hop, or hanging out under the grey towers of the city — California music was something different. It was outdoors, cars, the sky, the sea, and especially surfing.

Surfing music was born with the debut of "Surfin'," a local hit written by the Beach Boys — a group of high school boys from southern California comprised of brothers Brian, Carl, and Dennis Wilson; their cousin Mike Love; and eventually Al Jardine and Bruce Johnston.

When their first album, "Surfin' Safari," was released in November of 1962, they started a boom of California music that promoted the surfing craze through the works of groups like Jan and Dean, the Ventures, and the Surfaris — and a host of other groups capitalizing on the fad. The next big thing was cars, such as the Beach Boys' classics "Little Deuce Coupe" and "Shut Down." But the sound of California only began here. By 1965, the Byrds had begun to promote folk rock with their rendition of Bob Dylan's "Hey, Mr. Tambourine Man." The Beach Boys themselves began to go psychedelic with their unquestioned masterpiece, "Good Vibrations." And suddenly, in 1966, the texture and nature of rock music had changed from a folk music of urban America into an eclectic, intellectual style.

While the work of the British was getting all the artistic recognition in the media, with the Beatles' extraordinary records and the plethora of English groups, many of the essential innovations for which the Beatles were credited elicited more from the West Coast school of music than from Britain.

Much of the use of the studio as a recording instrument — which was accredited to the June 1967 "Sergeant Pepper" album — was actually precluded by one of America's most underrated and talented groups, the Beach Boys.

In recording "Good Vibrations" they used all the conventional

The Beach Boys's unquestioned masterpiece, "Good Vibrations," was released in October of 1966, and remains today one of the best examples of studio musicianship.

techniques of studio tape recording — multitrack recording, reverberations, echoes, fades, and time-delays. However, composer Brian Wilson began using these effects not only as an emphasis for a certain song or phrase, but also as a new musical vocabulary in itself. Wilson altered the very continuity of his music, using the Moog synthesizer and other sounds emanating from electronic or recording processes as new voices and instruments for music.

Their baroque use of counterpoint sound had been established on their previous, May 1966, "Pet Sounds" album; but with "Good Vibrations" they fully exemplified the new "studio" sound with its many overlapping voices and the musical disruption of normal continuity and melody. And today, "Good Vibrations" still stands out as the unquestioned standard of the "studio" sound and the best effect of psychedelic influences on rock 'n' roll — and the life style of psychedelia was just beginning.

Meanwhile, California had become a hotbed of creation for rock 'n' roll groups. Centered around two cities, Los Angeles and San Francisco, the action started in all the clubs and dance halls where new artists could perform, like the Fat Angel, the Whiskey A Go Go, the Troubador, and others around the Sunset Strip area. In San Francisco it was Bill Graham's Fillmore Auditorium, the Avalon Ballroom, and the Carousel. One article supposed that there were over 1,500 groups playing in the Bay Area of San Francisco alone.

In Los Angeles, the Doors ruled the city. Led by lead singer Jim Morrison, the Doors were a precedent-shattering group in those days who gave a new psychological approach to rock music. The group — comprised of Morrison, Ray Manzarek on organ, John Densmore on drums, and guitarist-songwriter Bobby Krieger — left many spellbound with their first album. Though it was "Light My Fire," written by Krieger, which was the smash single, it was an eleven-and-a-half-minute composition by Morrison called "The End," which won them acclaim.

A stream-of-consciousness number in something of a raga-flavored presentation, "The End" told of the impending end of a love affair, quite possibly by murder. Perhaps the first song in pop music to create true drama and catharsis, the piece ended with a passage of patricide and Oedipal love that literally stunned the public in live performance.

The Doors' many albums were all successful, and their public career glittered with arrests for inciting riots and public outrages. At the end of a violently flamboyant career, Jim Morrison, who always screamed and swirled through performances clad only in skin-tight black leather, died in his bathtub in Paris, in 1971.

Another superb West Coast talent whose life was sorrowfully short was Janis Joplin, whom many people acclaimed as the best blues singer since Bessie Smith. Joplin, who sang with a San Francisco band called Big Brother and the Holding Company, had a magnificent, powerful voice, and the wildest, most raw-edged sexuality of any female stage performer in decades. She would improvise on songs, teasing, flaunting her ragged, handsome body and wide-mouthed good looks at the audience — perhaps the only woman of rock who ever did to men what Elvis Presley and Mick Jagger did to women.

Janis Joplin and her band's first namesake bluesy, rock album was terribly recorded, and "Cheap Thrills" and "Kozmic Blues" were only close to her wild, lush talents. After her death in a West Coast motel room in 1970, her two posthumous albums, "Pearl" and "Joplin in Concert," finally captured her fantastic spirit.

The Grateful Dead, led by wizard guitarist Jerry Garcia, and composed of Phil Lesh on bass, Pig Pen McKernan on drums, Bob Weir on rhythm guitar, and various others from time to time, is a model of one rock 'n' roll band getting better through hard work and communal growth.

At the beginning they were a sort of house band for the Acid Test tripped-out dances at the Fillmore. Their first two albums were unsuccessful. When they played in public, one could dance to their music, but they were sloppy. Then, with "Workingman's Dead," they began to coalesce as songwriters and performers. That album was part of the late '60's country rock explosion. The Dead were prototypes, even splitting into a Jekyll-Hyde relationship as another band, New Riders of the Purple Sage — performing as two bands at the same concert, dividing the program into country rock and hard rock.

Other San Francisco groups during this period had a tendency toward a soft, harmonic style. The Mamas and the Papas sang a sort of baroque rock, with intertwining harmonies and lines that were some of the most compelling in rock. Hits like "California Dreamin'," "Monday, Monday," and "I Saw Her Again" became forever associated with a sunny, easy West Coast style of life.

More Bay Area groups of note were Steppenwolf, a hard rock group that found success late in the decade; Gary Puckett and the Union Gap, a sort of a teeny-rock band; the Association, which sounded like a vocal chorus; the rock assortment called Moby Grape, which demonstrated that overpromotion could get a record nowhere. The group only sold records after everyone started ignoring them. Country Joe and the Fish wrote and performed a style of country-protest-ragtime rock with great skill and humor, and Scott MacKenzie sang "San Francisco (Be Sure to Wear Some Flowers in Your Hair)" which was an anthem of the 1966 pilgrimage to the Haight-Ashbury district — the Mecca of the psychedelic movement.

Then there was the Jefferson Airplane. Actually the first San Francisco group to make it big — they were the first with a super hit, "Somebody to Love," and the first to receive a fat recording contract and national promotion. Their artistic and financial success sparked the rush to sign up any group from San Francisco who could get themselves together enough to show up for a recording date. And in those days — it wasn't all that easy.

The vocals were led by ex-model and singer-composer Grace Slick. On stage you really couldn't tell what was going on — they had such a free-form group, with Jorma Kaukonen on lead guitar; Jack Casady on bass; Spencer Dryden on drums; Paul Kanter on rhythm guitar; and Marty Balin on lead vocals. Their musical talents were formidably varied as well: they could play anything on stage — folk, blues, jazz, ragtime — they were a constant amazement and challenge to all.

In 1971, the Airplane formed their own company, Grunt Records, and began splitting into various elements. Kaukonen and Casady started singing country and rural blues as Hot Tuna, and other members of the group released single records as well. But they will always be remembered as the first of the big-name groups from San Francisco.

The last of the big-name groups was perhaps the Buffalo Springfield. Singing and writing exactly the same kind of music that was to sell millions of records only two years later, the Springfield in 1966–68 was a perfect example of a group that was playing a style of music ahead of its time.

Steve Stills played guitar, keyboards, and sang vocals; Neil Young sang and played lead guitar; Ritchie Furay played guitar and

Janis Joplin was a true performer — one of those people who seemed to be born inside out, with all her emotions exposed and available for all to see.

sang vocals; Jim Messina played bass; and Dewey Martin played drums. But except for the Stills' composition of "For What It's Worth," they did not have any hit records. And yet, if you listen to any of their three albums, you'll hear many of the same sounds and styles that made gold records for Crosby, Stills, Nash and Young in 1969.

In October of 1967, many of the original stores, dance halls, and businesses of the hippie movement started closing down, and that year winter snuffed out much of what was for years a national fount of peace and love. The following summer was one of hard drugs, riots, and murders for the San Francisco community. LSD was taken for granted — then ignored, and people began worrying about ecology, organic living, and going back to nature. The West Coast scene cooled off and nearly faded out.

The Grateful Dead played "acid rock" —
music composed of long free-form improvisations,
swirling and heavy feedback, fuzzy tones,
and lyrics that delved into the drug mystique.
As the New Riders of the Purple Sage,
the group played country rock.

ROCK 'N' ROLL
AS ART:
1966 TO 1968

There were three conspicuous changes in the world of popular music between 1966 and 1968. Foremost, rock 'n' roll was accepted as an art form, although most critics felt uneasy with the birthright of the music. They even softened up the term by calling the music simply "pop."

Secondly, there was an industrywide change in record sales from singles to long-playing albums. Part of this was due to the prosperity of the times. The economy was in an upswing inflation, and everybody seemed to have money to burn. So for a few dollars more, adults began to buy albums while kids aged twelve through seventeen bought the singles. Singles also remained big sellers in soul music.

Thirdly, again as a reflection of the boom economy of the period, record companies, in awe of the millions of records sold by such groups as the Beatles, began to sign artists left and right, and quickly created what record critics called "the great record glut." Toward the end of 1968, the output of the record industry quadrupled. Hundreds of new artists were shotgunned to the public. And hundreds of thousands of dollars were lost when mediocre groups were unsuccessful, and not a few important talents were lost in the shuffle.

Other conspicuous events during these two very important years were the development of genres of rock 'n' roll arranged by geographical location: the San Francisco sound, the New York sound, the Motown sound, and so on — just as blues had cooked different musical flavors in different urban stew pots. This was also the period of the second British invasion, which brought the classic acts of Cream, Jimi Hendrix, and the Who.

And coming full circle, were the blues and rock 'n' roll revivals of these years, which gave us artists like Paul Butterfield's Blues Band (who played pure rhythm and blues), the Blues Project, and Laura Nyro — all sometimes described as blue-eyed soul. In these two years, rock was seen to go full circle — from nonsense popular music to self-consciously intellectual art forms, back to a revival of the roots of rock 'n' roll and the blues.

During the period of 1966 to 1968 in America, anything was possible in popular music. And just about anything happened. It was a period often inspired and frequently induced by what began in San Francisco in 1966 as a summer of love and which shortly swept eastward to encircle the globe: the psychedelic revolution.

Psychedelic, which means "mind-manifesting," is a term used

to describe the effects of the consciousness-expanding (as some put it), or reality-altering drugs. They include depressants such as marijuana, stimulants such as amphethamine, and the true psychedelics, or hallucinatory drugs such as lysergic acid diethylamide (LSD), mescaline, and psycilocybin.

Soon it seemed as if everyone was trying the new sensation — drugs. Not that drugs were anything new to the musical scene. After all, music people have always been cursed with that extra level of energy that makes it possible for a performer to turn on an audience. Musicians have often taken many kinds of intoxicants from alcohol to the truly evil and dangerous hard drugs. Do they use them just to calm down? Some may, but there are always people predisposed to wrecking their lives. Whether it's smoking hashish until they can't play straight, or simply hitting the bottle, some people are always doomed to do foolish things. The best musicians seem to keep their escapes from reality under control and for short periods of time.

But it was the acid experience in the '60's that tended to influence music the most. The LSD experience distorts perceptions of time, space, and colors as we know them. Time elongates, stretches out to eternity; senses are mixed and confused; people taste colors, see music, and so forth.

Drugs were something new in 1966, so everyone was trying them. Thus it came about that "acid rock" was formed. This new music, however, included different styles. The Beatles' "Sergeant Pepper" album with its images and descriptions was one type, while the music of the Jefferson Airplane with its long, searching passages, full of harmonic distortion, fuzzy tones, and ecstatic high frequency screeches was another type. The music was infused with the sounds of Eastern instruments; it was music that lent itself to the trip.

Indian music is basically formal improvisation. Although the particular tunes sound unfamiliar to the Western ear, Indian music was just about the easiest thing for the tripped-out listener to follow! Then, too, it had the sense of suspense and wisdom, the surge of emotional passages leading to frequent climaxes. Rock music began showing the melodic patterns of Indian music influenced by master-musicians such as Ravi Shankar, Ali Akbar Khan, and others.

Huge amplifiers, their volumes turned all the way up, and electric instruments played hard and fast create much of the mood and feeling that characterizes acid rock.

68

*A scene from the
rock musical, Hair.*

From 1966 to 1968, Indian music could be found almost everywhere.

When George Harrison played the sitar in "Norwegian Wood," from the 1965 "Rubber Soul" album, it really began to catch on. Donovan used the sitar in "The Three Kingfishers" and Brian Jones of the Rolling Stones used it in "Paint It Black." Soon everyone was using every sort of instrument to complement rock tunes and lyrics.

By the end of 1965, America had seen practically everything the world of music had to offer spring up in various rock 'n' roll songs. To describe what happened during the years between 1966 and 1968 entails using such terms as acid rock, raga rock, jazz rock, blues rock, and any other combination of a formal music style with the word rock. But perhaps the easiest term is eclectic rock, a popular music that drew from all sources and musical styles to produce an explosion of musical ideas that was like a renaissance to rock 'n' roll.

One of the genuine signs that rock was being accepted by the artistic establishment during the late 1960's was the arrival of the rock musical — or Broadway musicals with rock songs and styles. The first was probably Tom Sankey's off-Broadway production of *The Golden Scew*, quickly followed by *Hair*, written by two actors, Gerome Ragni and James Rado, and set to music by a piano-bar composer, Galt MacDermot. *Your Own Thing* was next — a rock version of Shakespeare's *Twelfth Night*, and *Two Gentlemen of Verona*, another rock version of a Shakespearian play. This was 1967, but before long, rock was as familiar a sound to come from Broadway orchestra pits as a string section.

Many pseudo-religious musicals came next, from *Salvation*, to *Tarot*, to *Godspell* and finally — the extraordinarily flamboyant version of *Jesus Christ, Superstar*. All were successful ventures, with long lines and cheerful, if patronizing reviews. Rock had gone about as commercial as it could get.

Next, rock became almost classical, with the advent of musicals like *Grease*, which sings the songs of the '50's, struts the dances, and tells of the life styles of growing up in the Eisenhower era. Rock 'n' roll has almost become as much a classical form as English Repertory Theatre.

After a while, no one used the words "rock 'n' roll" to describe what was happening. They simply dropped all the prefixes entirely, and started referring to the new music as rock.

What were the highlights of these rock years? Perhaps one of the most outstanding characteristics was the intellectuality of the music.

71

People tried to create an art form with the new music, so the music became more lyrical and "head" oriented instead of rhythmical and "body" directed. People started to settle down in their seats. There was a great deal less dancing at concerts. Rock, with all its artistic desires, was now a music to listen to in depth.

The Beatles' albums were what really started the whole "rock as art" phenomenon. "Revolver," as mentioned earlier, released in August 1966, was the keynote for eclectic rock, with its elements of classical music, pop fun, and avant-garde jazz. Their next album was "Sergeant Pepper's Lonely Hearts Club Band" released in June of 1967. The critics went wild.

The Beatles made the Sergeant Pepper album the way most people make single recordings: the entire record was produced as a conceptual unity, a kind of "pop opera" (complete with a libretto — the lyrics appeared on the back cover). The album actually told a story. Sort of an "Acid Trip of Everyman," but with a pursuable plot and all forms of music from circus orchestration to '30's pop; from the baroque rock of "Rubber Soul" to the psychedelic rock of "Lucy in the Sky with Diamonds." Their masterpiece, "A Day in the Life," created the crescendo of all times with an entire orchestra playing each instrument simultaneously from the lowest note to the highest.

"Sergeant Pepper" was a prototype — a pattern for hundreds of albums to come — in the concept or story-telling tradition. Also, the album paved the way in using the recording studio as an instrument — in very much the same way the Beach Boys had done with "Good Vibrations." Now the technique was established: more groups began producing albums in the studio that could never be duplicated in live performance. In addition to cutting down on groups' live appearances, this trend contributed to a move away from the clean, simpler sounds of rock 'n' roll — and furthered the use-all-instruments, fool-around-in-the-studio trend. This gave rise to certain excellent works like Tom Rush's autobiography of a love affair, "The Circle Game," the Who's opera, *"Tommy,"* and *"Jesus Christ, Superstar."*

But then a time of mounting turmoil came for the Beatles as individuals. John Lennon married Yoko Ono, a Japanese filmmaker and artist; Paul McCartney started seeing Linda Eastman, an American photographer, and each of the Beatles began working on solo efforts, as first evidenced by the album in the plain white jacket: "The Beatles," which we will discuss later as it mirrored the back-to-simplicity and rock 'n' roll revival months of 1969.

For the Rolling Stones, the years between 1966 and 1968 were among the most trying in their history. Everywhere they went they were put down for their arrogant style — and finally Jagger and Richard were arrested for possession of marijuana. Later, in 1969, returning from Italy, Jagger was arrested again — but this time for possession of pep pills that he had purchased abroad legally. A huge public outcry arose, with the press pointing out that if Jagger had not been a rock star he would never have been arrested. He was finally acquitted on appeal.

Then in 1968, Brian Jones was arrested for possession of marijuana and released. In 1969, Jones quit the group for personal reasons, and died shortly thereafter of mysterious causes. The Stones held a huge wake for him in the middle of Hyde Park, and Jones was eventually replaced by Mick Taylor.

Musically, the Stones were releasing some of the best rock 'n' roll albums during these years — "Aftermath," "Between the Buttons," "Flowers," and "Their Satanic Majesties Request." Although they did not receive the critical acclaim that the Beatles enjoyed at this time, the Stones went on to become the top rock 'n' roll group of the '70's.

10

NEW
MOVEMENTS
IN ROCK

If by 1966 rock had achieved the status of art, by 1968 it was a religion or a cult of youth, a psychedelic life style. Rock was the hippies — the salvation or destruction of mankind, depending upon whose point of view you chose. Rock 'n' roll was the language of the hippies and everything they stood for: eternal youth, expanded consciousness, and either riches beyond imagination or a complete disregard for material success.

Yet the strange thing was that success was the standard for these times. These were the years of the superstars. People couldn't just play and compose good music. The new words were "charisma" and "heavy" — you had to have a flash of sainthood. The fast pace at which new stars were built up and then discarded (as we will see) led to a lot of instant has-beens.

The first major trend to break out of the ecstatic rock as art period when all those fantastic changes were taking place, when rock had finally grown up to the likes of Cream, Hendrix, and "Sergeant Pepper" was kiddie rock — rock music for those under the age of thirteen.

Kiddie Rock
Enter, the Monkees. They were four actors and singers put together as a singing group for a television show called "The Monkees." The group was an obvious imitation of the Beatles and the show itself, a takeoff on Beatles movies. But kids loved them, and they sold millions of records. It was rumored that some of the group only learned to play instruments after they had made their best-selling records — so they could perform in public. Their records, it is known, were often written by other people, with instrumentation played by studio musicians, and choruses sung by studio singers.

The people who put together the Monkees really started something. While the Monkees actually got better as they went along, other people started modeling groups on them. But then the people who put the Monkees together outdid themselves. They formed a group without singers, without instrumentalists, without bodies. The Archies were a group of cartoon characters from a television show — so anybody could contribute to their records. They had the number one hit single of 1969 — "Sugar." Most people who had been playing and singing on the road many years just turned away in disgust.

Then the trend turned toward young performers themselves.

Michael Jackson, the lead singer of the Jackson Five (a black family group), became a true star in the soul tradition. He started getting his first gold records when he was eight. Equally young were the child stars, the Osmond Brothers, whose lead figure Danny Osmond was a preteen singer in the white pop tradition. They sang the 1971 hit, "Go Away Little Girl." Then there's David Cassidy, who worked his way up through show business on television shows, culminating with "The Partridge Family." Recording with the cast of the television show (and resembling another singing family group of the late '60's, the Cowsills), he was the prominent figure in one of 1972's biggest sellers, "Cherish."

Radio Charts and Rock

Radio was clearly responsible for midwifing the birth of rock 'n' roll, as well as for naming it. In the mid-'50's and early '60's it was mostly AM radio with disc jockeys like Allen Freed and Murray "the K" Kauffman in New York, Tom "Big Daddy" Donahue in Philadelphia, Robin Seymour of Detroit, Hunter Hancock of Los Angeles, and Paul "Fat Daddy" Johnson of Baltimore.

These were the people who spread the faith of rock 'n' roll. Radio was pretty free in those days. Disc jockeys could play almost anything they wanted — but most programs had a "top forty" list of hits, which they would count down each week, or every day. Still, it was up to the disc jockey to decide which new songs he would play.

The "top forty" was usually a reflection of sales and listener interest in each radio station's area. All radio stations and many record stores across the country contributed their lists to the music industry trade papers — *Billboard*, then *Cashbox*, and *Record World* — for a compilation of the national charts of best-selling, and most-often-played records. These trade paper charts are still very important today, and they serve as the guide by which most stores order records.

In the 1960's, after the payola scandals, radio stations began getting more cautious about what they played, considering much of the new rock 'n' roll too daring for their stations. Consequently, play lists were started, and the records a disc jockey could play were generally decided on in conferences with radio station executives, or the program director himself.

Toward the middle of the 1960's, FM radio became more prominent, and started "free-form" or "alternate radio" programming, where individual disc jockeys could once again decide what they wanted to play. With the coming of the Beatles, the Doors, and other groups who recorded songs longer than the two to three minutes of most rock 'n' roll tunes up to this time, the FM stations started playing longer songs, and this meant albums instead of singles.

In the late '60's, along with the rock 'n' roll revival surge, there started a trend toward playing "oldies" — hits from the '50's and early '60's — on most AM and many FM radio stations. As the '70's began, more and more playlists were becoming the rule making it harder for new talent to get records played on radio. Unless a radio station plays a record you'll never hear it. It will not get exposure, and, because it's not being played on radio, your local store won't stock it. Without radio, the rock 'n' roll we know today would never have existed — without radio exposure it cannot grow or change.

Stage Scenes
Rock 'n' roll has always been a music of performance, a frequently visual as well as aural experience. The early pop idols, Frank Sinatra, Johnny Ray, and others first excited audiences because they showed their emotions on stage. When the first idol of rock came around — Elvis Presley — he was a whirlwind of emotion and demonstrative action, albeit preceded by energetic rhythm and blues performers for decades.

Little Richard tore up a storm, and Jerry Lee Lewis   the keyboards in front of his audience. But the 1960's were rather tame — the Beatles seemed to be having a lot of fun, but except for Lennon, they didn't dance like Chuck Berry, reel like B. B. King, or fly like James Brown. Only the Stones were wild on stage — and so received much public criticism. The heaviest mid-'60's work was being done on stage by the soul performers — of which Otis Redding knew no equal. Toward the end of the decade, the whites began to act up.

The Magic World of Arthur Brown lit bonfires on his crown, and ravaged the stage. The Who destroyed equipment and guitars. And Jimi Hendrix   his guitar to death and then set it afire. The Velvet Underground, the Doors, and the Stones brought a lot of whips and chains to the stage, and then came Dr. John, the Night Tripper, with his magical gris-gris dust, costumes, snakes, and dancing girls in vaporous clouds (he later turned out to be a very talented musical historian who also played a great variety of instruments).

With the turn of the decade, performances were pretty bizarre. For one thing, light shows — those swirls and patterns of colored light that would follow the movements of music with a psychedelic flash — were the rule behind any heavy rock act. But then things got really theatrical. The Incredible String Band brought in a mime troupe. The Bonzo Dog Band threw in every stage trick in the book — costumes, dances, funny instruments, and explosive effects — and finally, the Stooges and Alice Cooper appeared.

The Stooges played such a sadistic game that they actually flailed the flesh off themselves in performance. Leader Iggy Stooge would work up to such hysteria that he would rake nails across his bare chest and draw blood. They could empty a house quicker than any fire alarm.

But Alice Cooper reached a peak in the art of blowing minds from the stage. He dressed himself up as a sinister, scraggly girl, and then took on all the repulsive things in his imagination: he tore apart dolls representing babies, did the live snake number, and eventually staged his own mock hanging for the audience. The thing was, as with most of these seemingly outrageous acts — he was quite funny once you realized it was all an act.

In the early '70's, glitter rock became widespread. Performers like Marc Bolan, Elton John, and David Bowie brought a theatrical presentation, complete with elaborate costumes and heavy make-up, to their stage appearances.

And the music? For most of these groups the level was actually quite high on the scale of quality, but the most bizarre acts were the ones where you would generally hear the least music.

Festivals

The festival idea — getting hundreds of thousands of people together to see a large number of acts — probably started with the Greeks in some ancient theatre. It caught on in America with the country and classical music festivals given since the turn of the century. It has become a profitable concept with festivals like Tanglewood in the Berkshire Mountains of Massachusetts and the Newport Folk and Jazz Festivals in Rhode Island.

Then in the summer of 1969 came Woodstock: half a million people flocked to Woodstock, New York, to watch dozens of the world's best acts doing some of the best performances of their lives. Not that anyone cared; it was just too much — two major rainstorms and a lot of tripping, dope-smoking, and swimming in the nude. Helping each other out created a miracle: peace and music, just like the advertisements promised. For the kids, they had proved it

Despite pouring rains, mud,
food and drinking-water shortages,
illnesses, and overdoses of drugs,
rock music fans continued flocking
to the Woodstock festival.

could work: the hippie life style had triumphed. Dozens of festivals were scheduled.

But then came the Rolling Stones' free concert at Altamount, California. Three accidental deaths and a murder were caught on a film of the event, "Gimme Shelter." The Hells' Angels motorcycle gang had been hired for security, but created more trouble than any of the audience, and so the idea of festivals cooled — until the next year, when several were held, but none made money. Then in 1972, another round of festivals started. Festivals, it seemed, were here to stay — but they gradually became smaller and more controlled. The Woodstock phenomenon will probably never be duplicated.

Country Rock

Meanwhile, another trend had sprung up: rock and country western music. Before the end of 1969, the sound of those twangy Nashville guitar licks and the whine of the pedal steel guitar could be heard everywhere. Where did it start? Some say with the January 1968 release of Dylan's "John Wesley Harding," where in country-sounding songs he used a few Nashville studio musicians. Others think it was the influence of Glenn Campbell singing songs like "By the Time I Get to Phoenix," and "Gentle on My Mind." But after all, country rock had already been around for a while in the work of people like the Buffalo Springfield, the Byrds, and certainly Johnny Cash.

But then it became an explosion with groups like Poco and the Flying Burritos; and even Joan Baez recorded a country album. Soon everyone was sliding out those country and western tunes, and as mentioned earlier, the Grateful Dead/New Riders even split into two bands to accommodate their own twin interests in rock and country. With the release of Dylan's "Nashville Skyline," which he recorded entirely in Nashville — and sang one duet with Johnny Cash himself — country rock became another permanent style in the rock vocabulary.

Meanwhile, another two-sided movement was traveling the rock road: a combination of rock 'n' roll oldies with a blues revival. In the rock 'n' roll side of the occasion, people who hadn't worked for years at big money — Chuck Berry, Bo Diddley, Bill Haley and the Comets — were suddenly having joint concerts. And the kids were having dances in '50's clothes and hairstyles. Nothing happened on the nation's charts, but the concerts sold very well throughout the country.

The blues revival was more a part of the "heavy band" phenomenon. Cream was essentially a blues band, and they played everything from delta blues to '50's R & B. The Rolling Stones cut delta blues numbers on their November 1968 "Beggar's Banquet" album, as well as the 1969 "Let It Bleed." Then too, there were people like Johnny Winter, a white, albino blues guitarist from Texas, who was signed to a $400,000 recording contract by Columbia Records after an article appeared on him in *Rolling Stone Magazine.*

The Paul Butterfield Blues Band inspired many people who changed from folk to hard rock. This heavy rock trend continues as this is being written. While the Cream is generally credited with its beginning, another early heavy rock group was Led Zeppelin. They replaced the Beatles as number one group in the respected *Melody Maker Magazine* poll. All of their blues-oriented rock albums have gone gold. An unruly, boisterous act, Zeppelin is one of the few real crazies left in rock 'n' roll. Other groups in the heavy tradition — such as Black Sabbath and Grand Funk Railroad — are somewhat similar in their heavy-volumed, repetitive chords, and ominous bashed-out sound.

The breakup of Cream — they had a 1969 farewell tour — was a ball. No group ever had so much fun breaking up — or so much publicity in the process. It must have been catching, because as the New Year's Eve ball came bouncing down on Times Square in New York City at the dawn of 1970, a message came over the Allied Chemical Tower's electric ticker tape: Paul McCartney had declared that the Beatles were finished as a performing group.

Maybe it was the decline in the American economy that created a shortage of jobs and money. Whatever the cause, the scene in rock for 1970 was Splitsville. Groups started breaking up left and right.

Of course, artists have always wanted to perform solo, but it was the Beatles' breakup that was taken the hardest by the public. How could four lads who were the best of everything want to part? For them, it was easy. For one thing, since "Magical Mystery Tour," the Beatles had not really been a group as they were before. The album that followed, entitled "The Beatles" and known as the "White Album" for its plain jacket, was a series of individual songs. Every track was Lennon and the band; McCartney and the band, etc. Also, everyone was getting married and starting to lead lives separate from the group. As could be seen in the film, "Let It Be," nobody was getting along too well.

Still, their following albums, "Let It Be" and "Abbey Road," were terrific. But then they started doing solo albums. John Lennon starting first with Yoko Ono in 1969, released   followed by many others, including four gold records. Paul McCartney and Linda Eastman began with "McCartney," "Ram," and "Wild Life" — all of which went gold as immediate million-dollar sellers. George Harrison came out with his three record set of "All Things Must Pass," including his superhit single, "My Sweet Lord"; and Ringo Starr released "Sentimental Journey" and "Beaucoups of Blues," with his hit single, "It Don't Come Easy." Each of the Beatles was getting his own gold records and not complaining too much after the initial split, though in the beginning they would quarrel with each other in recorded messages sprinkled through their albums, such as Lennon's "How Can You Sleep?"

One group that actually got together in 1969 — after splitting from others, of course — came out with one of the most influential albums in recent years. David Crosby, Stephen Stills, and Graham Nash all sang and played guitar, with Stills and Nash playing keyboards as well. Stephen Stills, in fact, played almost all instruments and also arranged the music. The album, "Crosby, Stills & Nash," altered the course of rock music almost single-handedly. Curiously, it was closer to folk rock than any other single style of music. An extraordinary album, it had harmonies, lyrics, and a level of talent that was astonishing. The music was light, full of energy and intelligence. In many ways it represented the back-to-nature thinking of the new generation. No longer interested in heavy drugs and wild living, youth had become interested in ecology, trying to change the system from within, and trying to establish a calmer, healthier life style.

Crosby, Stills and Nash, later joined in 1970 by Neil Young, played mostly acoustic music in their first two albums. They added electric instruments only with care and good taste. Crosby, Stills, Nash and Young opened the way for more acoustic talents, and so genuine folk singers like James Taylor, Joni Mitchell, Kris Kristofferson, and soft-rock singers like Cat Stevens, Van Morrison, Neil Diamond, and Melanie became popular. Pop singers also had a chance in the new wave, with tunesmiths like Carly Simon, Leonard Cohen, Tim Hardin, and the Carpenters selling well in a slightly depressed market.

Then 1971 seemed to be the year of the pianist, with Carole King, Elton John, and Lee Michaels striking gold. King, a fantastic songwriter responsible for such '60's tunes as "A Natural Woman" and "Will You Still Love Me Tomorrow?" was named artist of the year for 1971 by the National Academy of Recording Arts and Sciences

Crosby, Stills, Nash and Young.
A band comprised of very talented individuals,
they have all made solo albums
as well as group albums.

for her album, "Tapestry." Elton John, a British singer-pianist, landed one Gold Record after another, and seems to be in constant danger of overexposure, since he was such an overnight superstar.

On the soul frontier, the faith has been kept by Sly and the Family Stone, with one gold album after another, and an unusual reputation for rarely showing up to give a concert. Ike and Tina Turner are another soul duo who have enjoyed much success. Aretha Franklin has been a solid gold mine of million-sellers throughout this period; and another singer, Roberta Flack, who was trained in classical piano, is making it both on the soul and pop charts — with every one of her records to date certified gold. Smokey Robinson and the Miracles, Marvin Gaye, James Brown, and Diana Ross have also kept a-truckin'.

Then there have been some originals added to the rock family. The husky-voice blues follower Rod Stewart has sprung out of his group, Faces, to become one of the most prominent superstars of the day. Latin rock has been pioneered as well during this period with the work of such groups as Santana and Malo.

And groups keep splitting up. Stephen Sills, David Crosby, Graham Nash, and Neil Young have all made solid gold solo efforts. Each seems to have a new band at this writing — with Crosby and Nash a duo — and they continue to compose and record the very best music in the folk country rock traditions.

Jazz rock at last became a reality as jazz itself reappeared with Miles Davis, John McLaughlin and the Mahavishnu orchestra, Tony Williams, and others. Groups such as Emerson, Lake, and Palmer, Jethro Tull, Yes, King Crimson, Chase, and Blood, Sweat, and Tears actually succeeded in bringing true jazz onto the best-seller charts and into the nation's concert halls.

But what about good old rock 'n' roll? It's alive and well — and personified in the greatest rock 'n' roll band of all times: the Rolling Stones. Oh, there were quite a few others during this four-year period — Derek and the Dominos, Leon Russell, and the Allman Brothers. But these years seem to have been first and foremost, Stones years.

The Stones fulfilled all the expectations of "Satisfaction" and their early rock songs during the period of 1968 to 1972. With all their albums, they have made us respond to their music and given us the same primitive feeling and movement that has been unique to rock 'n' roll from the very beginning. Not only have they stuck together for ten years, they are a monument to the durability of rock.

The Rolling Stones.
Their music still pulsates
with the beat of
good ol' rock 'n' roll.

Many new rock talents are cropping up all the time. Rock continually goes through periods of change with deep swoops back into the blues roots — and as appears now, the music is once again lifting from a blues revival period and soaring to new heights of originality.

Since the very beginning of rock, people have always dismissed it as a music about to die. Psychiatrists described it as a "communicable disease" and worse in 1957. But by 1967, every major magazine had a rock 'n' roll critic on its staff. In the late 1960's, with the deaths of Hendrix, Joplin, and Morrison, people again said rock was through. Next, people thought the music had gone all pop — and the only real music was to be heard in the revival concerts. With the soft music trend at the turn of the '70's, people thought rock was a goner once again. Bill Graham closed his Fillmore theatres in New York and San Francisco with the statement that rock was finished as a business.

When you are listening to your radio as you read this — whenever in the future it may be — try to associate what you hear with what you have read in this book about traditional rock 'n' roll. Knowing where the music comes from can help you understand it, and give you that flash of enjoyment from new, hard-to-understand music that only comes with wisdom.

And then — perhaps more important than understanding it with your head — try and move to it. Even if the music is slow and deliberate, you can still relate to it with your body — because that's where it all comes from: the rhythms and movements of our very lives. And as long as people live, laugh, weep, make love, and breathe — in the 1955 words of Danny and the Juniors — "Rock and Roll Is Here to Stay."

SUGGESTED READINGS

Belz, Carl. *The Story of Rock*. New York: Harper Colophon Books, 1969.

Cohn, Nik. *Rock From the Beginning*. New York: Stein & Day, 1969.

Eisen, Jonathan, ed. *The Age of Rock*. New York: Vintage Books, 1969.

Gillett, Charlie. *The Sound of the City: The Rise of Rock and Roll*. New York: Outerbridge & Dienstfrey, 1970.

Keil, Charles. *Urban Blues*. Chicago: University of Chicago Press, 1966.

Robinson, Richard. *Electric Rock*. New York: Pyramid Books, 1971.

Roxon, Lillian. *Lillian Roxon's Rock Encyclopedia*. New York: Grosset's Universal Library, 1971.

Shaw, Arnold. *The Rock Revolution*. New York: Paperback Library, 1971.

———. *The World of Soul*. New York: Paperback Library, 1971.

Traum, Artie and Happy. *Rock Guitar*. New York: Amsco Music Publishing Co., 1969.

ALL OF THE ABOVE ARE AVAILABLE IN PAPERBACK

INDEX